DAN R. DICK

*Rethinking
Conventional
Wisdom
about
Church
Leadership*

Abingdon Press
Nashville

BURSTING THE BUBBLE
RETHINKING CONVENTIONAL WISDOM ABOUT
CHURCH LEADERSHIP

Library of Congress Cataloging-in-Publication Data

Dick, Dan R.
    Bursting the bubble : rethinking conventional wisdom about church leadership / Dan R. Dick.
       p. cm.
    ISBN 978-0-687-46513-2 (pbk. : alk. paper)
    1. Christian leadership. I. Title.

BV652.1.D525 2008
253—dc22

2008025620

08 09 10 11 12 13 14 15 16 17—10 9 8 7 6 5 4 3 2 1
MANUFACTURED IN THE UNITED STATES OF AMERICA

For Carl Andry,
who taught me never to take anything at face value

For Neill Hamilton,
who taught me that
there is always more to every story

For anyone and everyone
who values critical thinking

And for Barbara,
who thinks I have something of value
to share with the church

This book is for you

CONTENTS

COULD EVERYTHING WE KNOW BE WRONG?

On my first day of Old Testament class in 1977, our professor tossed his copy of the Tanak on the desk, looked at us, and said, "You may think you know a lot about the Hebrew Scriptures, but hear this—everything you know is wrong." He assigned us a few chapters in our textbook, got up, and left the room. I remember being annoyed—angry even—but this event stays clear in my mind, and over the course of thirteen weeks, he pretty well proved his point. There was another side to almost everything I had ever heard or learned about the "Old Testament" (including calling it the Old Testament). Much of what I held to be fact was wrong, incomplete, inaccurate, or a well-intentioned lie. The greatest gift I received from the class was permission and encouragement to bring the best of critical thinking to issues of religious belief, theology, Christology, and all things church related. For the past thirty years I have dedicated myself to looking at multiple sides of any issue, questioning conventional wisdom, and seeking as many different perspectives as possible.

It is obviously improper to proceed under the impression that everything we know is wrong. Instead, let us proceed with the *possibility* that much of what we know is incomplete, inaccurate, or founded more in myth than fact. This is not to imply that people are gullible but merely to point out that human beings make decisions and form beliefs from the information that is available to them. When bad or incomplete information spreads, it becomes conventional wisdom—what everybody "knows." This book is an assault on conventional wisdom. It confronts what everybody "knows" to say "yes, but . . ." It is intended to supplement incomplete information with other relevant facts. It challenges inaccurate information with basic common sense. It shines the light of critical thinking on mythological messages and misguided marketing. It happily pokes holes in the arguments of popular theories and trends in mainline Protestant and independent evangelical Christianity. It is a pathway through a lot of confusing data and information to identify and name the critical issues confronting our church today. And by God's grace, it will offer suggestions to cutting through the mass of misinformation to help church leaders chart a viable course into the future.

What this book doesn't mean to do is to criticize people for what they believe and think they know. This is not an "I'm smarter than you are" kind of book but rather a careful analysis of where our thinking breaks down. The human brain is apparently designed to make meaning and bring order out of chaos.[1] The mind processes random bits of data and information, seeking patterns, connections, and associations. This is how we make sense out of our world. However, every human being receives incomplete input at the very least. There are gaps in the information we receive. No matter, though, for our reasoning brains are designed to fill in the gaps—to make leaps of faith, assumptions, and inferences to help us create knowledge.

When we talk about knowledge, we often think we're talking about facts, not beliefs; truth, not opinion. However, much of what we "know" is predicated on what we think, believe, conjecture, or assume. Learning theorists developed a concept called the ladder of inference to help illustrate this normal aspect of human reasoning.

For example, you see a colleague, call her Tiffany, coming into the office one morning. You smile and greet Tiffany, but she just looks at you with a frown and slightly shakes her head as she passes. You immediately ask yourself, *What's wrong with Tiffany?* Then you remember, you owe Tiffany ten dollars you borrowed for lunch two weeks ago and forgot about. She must be upset about not getting her money back. (First rung on the ladder of inference—assuming you know something you don't.) Oh, my gosh, she'll never trust you again! (Second rung—projecting intention or predicting reaction.) Well, I'd better stay out of her way until I can pay her back and apologize. (Third rung—changing behavior based on what you have decided must be true.) In fact, Tiffany just had an argument with her fiancé in the car, is not feeling overly friendly at the moment, but would love more than anything a sympathetic ear to listen to her troubles. The ladder of inference causes us to drift farther and farther from the truth, all the while making us think we know more than we did before. This process works constantly in human beings and lays the foundation for conventional wisdom.

There are many problems with conventional wisdom, not the least of which is that it simply means that often the loudest voice is assumed to be the most reliable. An example in our current American culture is the myth of the liberal media. Everyone hears all the time that the United States is defined by a liberal media bent on pushing the liberal agenda to a conservative country. Where does this message come from? If the media is liberal, why would it complain about itself being liberal? Who has the most to gain by pointing out that the media is liberal? Political and religious conservatives Bill O'Reilly, Ann Coulter, Rush Limbaugh, Laura Schlessinger, Pat Robertson, Pat Buchanan, Cokie Roberts, George Will, and on and on, all have prominent voices in contemporary American "liberal" media. They yowl endlessly about the biased media. The entire argument is based on an assumed gullibility of the American public. First, it argues that the media is one, discrete thing. Second, it assumes that a single minority dominates the whole. Last, it denies that a third mind-set—that of the moderate—exists, and that this third mind-set is the dominant segment (approximately two-thirds of Americans place themselves in the moderate category).[2] The myth of the liberal media is hardly even questioned—the ubiquity of the phrase must make it true—even when someone like Karl Rove is hired by *Newsweek* magazine.

This is a condition of our modern American culture—speak loudly and long enough, and opinion becomes fact. Gain enough influence, and whatever you say can shape the thinking of millions. Celebrity trumps credentials every time. Oprah Winfrey can influence what books are read, what music is heard, what television shows and movies are watched, and what pop celebrities are heeded.

By her acknowledgment and approval, writers, artists, and professionals unable to achieve success by their own merits and efforts can (and do) become overnight sensations. Oprah can proclaim "Good!" and it becomes so; she can condemn "Bad!" and literally millions of people agree. Is Oprah smarter than everyone else? Is her opinion that much more valid and well informed than yours or mine? Of course not, but that's beside the point. The Oprah mystique is much larger than Oprah—it doesn't have its basis in rational thinking or worthiness. Oprah is one of those rare individuals that Malcolm Gladwell calls "connectors."[3]

In bygone days, priests and politicians were the key influencers in many cultures. Potentates, philosophers, presidents, professors, and pastors were the learned individuals who set the course for people's thoughts and behaviors. Today, businessmen, bloggers, and Britney Spears wield more clout than teachers and other public servants in shaping public opinion. The only way a political leader can exert real power is by first achieving the status of media celebrity. What is known and what we believe we know become more and more confused all the time. The inundation of information causes us to think we know more than we actually do because information is not knowledge. Information, at its best, is the stuff of which knowledge is made. When we sift and sort through all the facts, factoids, bits, bytes, data, detritus, trivia, and trumpery for the few gems of real information, we begin to piece together ideas, concepts, and wisdom with lasting value and practical application. By our testing and refining of this information over time, true knowledge emerges. But in our "need it yesterday," "immediate gratification isn't fast enough," "don't confuse me with the facts" modern culture, we don't take the time to test, challenge, refine, or perfect information—and what we know suffers a dereliction of quality.

Many factors affect this trend toward knowledge decay, a number of them exacerbated by the baby boom generation (of which I am a member). Of all the people living on the planet earth in the twenty-first century, Americans born between 1946 and 1964 seem to hold one of the most limited, selfish, shortsighted, and impenetrable worldviews imaginable. This worldview manifests itself in four distinct conceits:

1. If it happened before we were born, then it isn't worth paying attention to.
2. If it happens anywhere else but the United States, it is inferior.
3. If it didn't happen to us personally, then it is irrelevant.
4. If it isn't on television, then it didn't really happen.

Of course, other factors describe and define the baby boom generation—as many positive as negative, in fact—but those most affecting our view of reality and what we "know" are those listed above. And while these are cultural phenomena, their impact on the Christian church in America, in all its many forms, is immense. Each of these boomer conceits will provide lenses for analysis of the state of the modern American church and challenges to our ecclesial conventional wisdom.

The problem in attacking the conventional wisdom in the contemporary church is not in finding something to assess but in figuring out where to begin. There are so many dominating and distracting myths in mainline and evangelical America that are deeply connected to each other, that knowing which ones are most deceptive is difficult.

Is the myth of membership decline more important than the myth of generational theory? Is the fallacy of the megachurch more of a problem than the supposed moral decay of America? What about postmodernism, the emergent church, the mosaic generation, contemporary worship, clergy misconduct, homosexuality, and Purpose-Driven-What-Would-Jesus-Do-Prosperity-Gospel-Prayer-of-Jabezism? And what about the more practical problems of bad pastoral leadership, not enough money, too much staff and property, and the rising costs of insurance? We all know the church is going to hell in a collection basket, unless you're a celebrity pastor-CEO running a Wal-Martesque megachurch, don't we? We also know that some church growth guru or megachurch superstar will write the book of books, replacing the Bible as the key to success, salvation, and the very kingdom of God. It's just a matter of time.

This book is a gentle nudge—a wake-up shake on the shoulder—to say, "Hey, there's more to this story than what we've been fed by the media, the markets (church and secular), and the modern myth-mongers who jack up the ecumenical terror alert to orange, magenta, and scarlet." It is a call to common sense; an invitation to apply the basic principles of critical thinking to myriad messages that simply are not true. It is meant as a missive of hope that there is more to almost every story, and what we don't know is even better than what we do know (or think we know).

This book has five sections. Section One—"Getting with the Times"—examines conventional wisdom concerning the modern era in four short chapters: "Lacking a Sense of History," "Boomer Boo-Boo: The Problem with Generational Theory," "Postmodernism: The Day after Tomorrow Yesterday," and "Critics, Critics Everywhere, but Not a Thought to Think." The second section—"Mine Is Bigger Than Yours"—explores what it means to be a church in modern America with the chapters "Megachurch Megamyths," "The Pastor: Direct Line to the Man (Person) Upstairs," "How Low Can You Go? (Expectations, That Is)," "Cloning Pastor Happy," and "Mortgaging the Mission." Section

Three—"Getting the Word Out"—shifts focus to the work of the church in chapters titled "The Medium Is the Message," "Vampire Christianity," "Faith Shoving: The New Evangelism," and "Überfaith versus Interfaith." Section Four—"Missing the Point"—surveys popular trends and hot-button issues in the church: "Emergent Detergent" and "Something Old, Something New, Something Borrowed, Something Blue." The conclusion—"Getting Over Ourselves"—calls on church leaders to reevaluate key questions: WWJRDIHWTCBT? (What Would Jesus *Really* Do If He Were to Come Back Today?), The World Still Needs the Church, The Church Still Needs the World, and Does the Church Still Need Us? These titles are primarily meant to be humorous, not inflammatory or obnoxious—though obnoxious is in the nose of the beholder. None of the problems facing the Christian church today will be solved if God's people lack a sense of humor. The problems are serious, our faith is serious, the needs are serious, and the time is urgent—all excellent reasons for us to lighten up.

Notes

1. Research in and knowledge of the human brain change almost daily, but a current, enjoyable exploration of the way our brains work is Sandra Aamodt and Sam Wang's *Welcome to Your Brain: Why You Lose Your Car Keys But Never Forget How to Drive and Other Puzzles of Everyday Life* (New York: Bloomsbury, 2008).
2. The Gallup Poll "How Different Groups of Americans Plan to Vote on Nov. 7" (Sept. 13, 2006) indicates that while 37 percent of voters consider themselves "conservative," and 21 percent consider themselves "liberal"—leaving 42 percent in the "moderate" category—16 percent of conservatives align their views with more moderate voters, while among liberals, those leaning toward moderate are an additional 24 percent. All in all, the "moderate" or middle-of-the-road perspective constitutes a sizable majority.
3. Malcolm Gladwell, *The Tipping Point* (Boston: Little, Brown & Company, 2000), pp. 38–54.

GETTING WITH THE TIMES

Modern American culture poses interesting challenges to the Christian faith. It is a fascinating time to be alive and to listen to all the different perspectives about contemporary Christianity. Some voices claim we are in a completely new place, experiencing things that no one else has ever faced before, while others say that the Christian church at the beginning of the twenty-first century very closely resembles the Christian movement of the first century. Some social commentators reframe the culture in terms of generational theory, attempting to describe and define entire groups of people to help us plan for the future and strategize for today. Many prominent voices across the church borrow the language and philosophical constructs of postmodernism in an attempt to better understand and explain the present day. There is also confusion about the role that Christianity plays in the larger cultural context of America—one segment claiming that we are a Christian nation, the other protesting that Christianity is under attack.

One thing is clear—the church still matters, and religion is as hot today as it has ever been (in all its varied forms). It is almost impossible to turn on the television, surf the Web, or browse a magazine or newspaper and not encounter issues of a religious nature. Whether you are for it or against it, it is virtually impossible not to talk about religion.

This is nothing new. But the scope and the reach of the discussion have changed. What used to be discussed face-to-face at home or at work is now a topic for global discourse. Cable television and the Internet make formerly personal and private opinions public property. Some think this trend is fantastic, allowing everyone equal voice in issues of life and death, meaning and purpose. Others decry the fact that ill-informed opinion now has equal clout with well-studied knowledge and critical thinking.

It really doesn't matter whether it is good or bad. Where we are is where we are, and if we want to remain relevant in the days to come, we need to get with the times.

CHAPTER 1

LACKING A SENSE OF HISTORY

 "We are living in a unique time of unprecedented change. No culture has ever faced the challenges that we face today. History will look back on this era as the most innovative of all time." Give me a break. Any time a book begins this way, I want to chuck it across the room. It is evidence of one thing and one thing only—the author has no sense of history. If he or she did, he or she would realize that authors have been starting their books and articles this way for centuries. Every age is unique. Every age is characterized by the monumental changes that define it. History does look back in amazement. So what?

Does anyone really believe that the computer, the Internet, cell phones, iPods, MRIs, and bottled water have a greater impact on people today than electricity, the telephone, air travel, indoor plumbing, and the polio vaccine had nearly a century ago? Is the fact that change is happening so fast that much more impressive than the rate at which our coping mechanisms (for good and for ill) are increasing as well? Is it so hard to grasp that news stories aren't happening more often today than they did a century ago, but the amount of reporting has changed? The fact is, everything we are dealing with today has very similar and direct antecedents.

One case in point: gun violence in public schools. Many Americans fear that we are standing on the verge of an epidemic as malcontented and misunderstood youth take guns to school to do violence to teachers and classmates. However, as a percentage of the U.S. population, teenagers in school are safer now than they were in the 1920s. Why? Because it was not unusual for children to take hunting rifles and knives to school with them in the kinder, gentler America we believe once existed. Certainly, the technology of an old single-shot hunting rifle isn't as destructive as a semi-automatic NRA-approved assault rifle, but the incidence of gun violence is actually lower today, not higher. Why doesn't the media report this? Guess. Could it be that news isn't about information anymore, but is all about ratings and entertainment? We live in a culture of fear, and fear depends on ignorance, and too much helpful information prevents fear, so . . .

An analysis of many social ills reveals similar findings. A perusal of popular magazines of the 1930s and 1950s is an education in itself.[1] Topics include teen pregnancy, abortion, drug abuse, adultery, murder, gangs, premarital sex, birth control, and voyeurism. A large number of Americans are under the impression that these things are relatively new problems and that somehow the morals and values of our culture have decayed from those of a purer, healthier, and happier time. Students of history know it isn't necessarily true. Every social ill we face today is the progeny of a long line of social ills from the past. Teenagers in Civil War days drank, smoked, and drugged (home-grown corn likker, hemp, and opium); in my grandfather's day it was bathtub gin, roll-your-owns, and hashish; and in my own (don't tell anybody) it was Annie Green Springs, Lucky's, and pot. The medium changed but the methods, not so much.

Sexual promiscuity and experimentation follow a similar pattern. What has changed is not the practice but the penchant for publicity. Everybody talks about it now, whereas people kept silent before. One of the great aspects of my education was spending time with flapper-era, Jazz Age men and women in nursing homes and getting them to tell me of their less-than-devout exploits as young men and women. The stories are both shocking and a bit reassuring. People were people then too. We're not on a slippery slope toward moral depravity and destruction—at least, no worse than the one dear old mom and dad were on.

This lack of historical perspective finds purchase in the church as well as in the dominant culture. Leaders across Christendom would like nothing more than to make us believe that we are standing on the brink of a new age—a place unknown and unexplored by those who have come before. It is common and unfounded rhetoric that we are witnesses to the end of the age of Christendom (an amorphous golden era where Christians called the shots and religious leaders were respected and revered by everyone) and that we face a unique challenge because a corrupt and ungodly culture is out to get us. Poor us.

It's easy to see how people might believe we are living at the end of the Christendom era—as long as they haven't read a book from the past four hundred years or heard of the industrial age or the scientific revolution (essentially, modern times). The centrality of Christianity as arbiter of reality and the almost universal respect and regard of the priest and pastor have been in steady decline since the Protestant Reformation and the invention of movable type— which put the Bible in the hands of us rabble. Toss in Newton, Copernicus, and Galileo displacing heavenly intervention with physical and natural laws, and further erosion occurred. The lack of respect by authors such as Voltaire, Dickens, Thomas Paine, Nathaniel Hawthorne, Sinclair Lewis, and oh, about two thousand other writers through the last few centuries casts suspicion on the reverence idea. Spending ten minutes in any history section of the public library (yes, these libraries still exist) yields entertaining and sometimes embarrassing portraits of religion through the Middle Ages and Enlightenment.[2] While poor Charles Darwin takes all the heat for his theory of evolution through natural selection—the favorite target of modern-day religious leaders to show how hostile science is to God—Charles Lyell's claim that the earth was millions of years old (in 1830, twenty-nine years before Darwin's bombshell) got biblical scholars all bent out of shape. Interestingly, neither Lyell nor Darwin upset most nineteenth-century pastors, who immediately took the findings of science to point to the greatness of God rather than the inadequacy of the Bible.

Thousands of other examples confirm that unless you are about three hundred years old, you have not witnessed the end of Christendom. It ended a long time ago, and besides, the kind of respect and reverence expected is earned, not assumed. If the church wants to gain the respect of the world, it might want to clean up its act.

Regardless of the historical perspective, it is a safe claim to make that we live in a cynical and skeptical culture. Few people would argue that pastors receive less respect today than they did even a generation ago. But what profession does receive the same (or better) regard? It is part of our cultural makeup to be suspicious of people in power positions. We don't respect lawyers, doctors, politicians, government leaders, professors, or police officers as we once did. Why should pastors be any different?

As to the idea that we Christians are an endangered species, there is little evidence that is true. In a country where more than 90 percent claim to believe in a higher power, 86 percent call that higher power God, and three out of four people claim a Christian affiliation, it is growing ever harder to cry foul and pretend that we are the victims of a plot to overthrow God. Loud-mouthed Christo-celebrities may whine that Christmas is under fire and that liberals are trying to shut us down, but that is just a ploy to generate ratings. Christianity is not receiving a bad reputation because of its opponents; it is losing credibility because it is failing to live up to its hype.

Mainline denominations are in a snit because people aren't flocking into our buildings on Sunday morning anymore. We are scared to death that the decline in our membership will continue unabated until the day we close our doors and auction our buildings to the highest new-Christian bidder. But the Christian population worldwide is more than 2 billion—one-third of the entire population. There are more Christian churches in the United States than ever before. The praying and Bible-reading populations, according to Gallup and Barna, are just as strong as ever. How is it possible that we are growing and declining at the same time?

It just may be that all our talk about Christian unity and the oneness of the body of Christ is just that—talk. The problem isn't that Christianity is losing ground but that individual "flavors" of Christianity have gone flat. The United Methodist Church is losing market share to conservative and evangelical churches. Presbyterian and Lutheran churches have been losing their members at about the same rate, but they had fewer to lose to begin with. United Methodism and the various Baptist traditions distinguished themselves early on as evangelical in the classic sense—they were incredibly good at shaping and sharing a gospel message of invitation. It was real, it was personal, it was heartfelt, and it wasn't delivered in thirty-second spots on cable television. Mainline Protestants are not much good at evangelism anymore, and the emerging movements that are better at it are leaving us in the dust.

And this is as it should be. As difficult as it is to admit, most mainline denominations in America are last year's news. Our birth stories were similar—the old guard was inward focused, building buildings, professionalizing the pastorate, and positioning itself for a long, comfortable future. Young upstarts—like Baptists and Methodists—jumped on the opportunity. They aimed not at the head but at the heart, touching people's emotions with a message of God's love delivered to their street corner. The Second Great Awakening was not a return to tradition but new wine in new skins. The movements flourished, but as with all new movements, they had to be supported by structure and organization. They became, as a friend of mine once said, "first institutionalized, then constitutionalized, before ending up prostitutionalized."[3] As we view the trajectory of the twentieth century until today, all we see is that we are having done unto us as we once had done unto others. Pentecostalism, the Jesus movement, the growth of the parachurch (such as Campus Crusade, Young Life, and so on), the megachurch phenomenon, and the emergent movement are all variations on a theme. They are nothing new at the core, just new presentations of an age-old cycle.

Without a clear sense of history, we are indeed doomed to repeat it. Opening our eyes to the last 150 years, we can see at least three distinct and important lessons to learn as we move into our future. First, new movements and congregations are not enemies to attack. If there is any validity to a life cycle and natural evolution of religious movements, then there is nothing to gain by fighting change. Perhaps we don't like or appreciate what the newer movements bring, and, yes, they may threaten our livelihood and eminence into the future, but they have the right to enter the playing field. Second, there is nothing to be gained by abandoning our identity, heritage, and mission to try to compete head-to-head with new religious movements. They are succeeding because they appeal to a different group of people. When we go chasing after new audiences, trying desperately to get them to like us, we alienate our longtime adherents, and we miss the opportunity to connect with those seeking what we have to offer. Last, a picture is worth a thousand words. If there truly is unity in Christ, if the Christian life is in any way fundamentally superior to life without Christ, and if our counter-cultural message is that together we're stronger than we are apart, then we need to model a radical ecumenism that looks past the differences to forge new networks and partnerships for transforming ministry into a new age.

To be honest, size does matter. We want a church that attracts a new and ever expanding audience—but we want the character of this audience to resemble that of Jesus Christ. The world does not need more inert, inactive, unmotivated believers in Jesus Christ. We need leaders—preachers, evangelists, prophets, and teachers—who hold us to a higher standard. Our world needs the grace and power of the incarnate Christ, not merely a mob of Christian spectators. Too often our attention is on how we can compensate for all we lack—for the members lost and those yet unchurched—instead of strategizing powerful ways to capitalize on all we have—2 billion believers worldwide. It seems to make sense that 2 billion people could make a rather impressive impact on the greatest challenges of our age, were we able to get our act together.

Christendom does not have to be over, but it must be rebuilt. If Christianity is to be a world-changing force for good, it has to begin at home. History has much to teach us, and if we're willing to learn the lessons it offers, perhaps we can waste less time doing what has already been done and instead create something new, better, and lasting. Perhaps we can set aside our differences long enough to build collaborative friendships around the values and beliefs we hold in common. Maybe, just maybe, we could cease striving to defeat and destroy our "enemies" and instead celebrate the rich tapestry of brothers and sisters of many faiths and traditions seeking to find mercy, justice, peace, and love just as we are.

Notes

1. Especially periodicals like those published by EC (Entertaining Comics) in the 1950s. These publications incurred the wrath of educators such as Fredric Wertham, who crusaded to have comic books banned for their contribution to juvenile delinquency. EC tackled virtually any topic, and those topics provide an excellent window into the pure, moral world of 1950s America.
2. One such foray brought to my attention *The Elizabethan Underworld* by Gamini Salgado (London: Folio Society, 2005) that delightfully shows how little reverence and respect religious leaders deserved in the sixteenth century. The behavior of priests and monks was less than Christlike, to say the least.
3. One of the most wonderfully Christian and spiritual men I ever knew, Carl Andry, was also one of the most abrasive, irascible, irreverent, and philosophically cynical people I have ever had the privilege to know. I miss him a lot.

CHAPTER 2

BOOMER BOO-BOO

THE PROBLEM WITH GENERATIONAL THEORY

I was born in 1958. That makes me a baby boomer. Yippee! Almost everything that has happened in the past fifty years has been, basically, all about me. Following the end of World War II—and in the ensuing eighteen years (1946–1964)—America was transformed, both for good and for ill. In the generation following the war (thanks in part to Dr. Benjamin Spock), little children became the most prized possession in the United States. American couples popped out children almost as fast as was humanly possible. Our little psyches were protected, we were nurtured, the rod was spared and we were spoiled, public schools and public education became a high priority, and extracurricular activities boomed. We were 4-H'd, Scouted, Junior Achieved, sock-hopped, prommed, jocked, cheerled, and performing-arted like never before. Churches boomed as well, redesigning facilities and programs around Sunday school rooms, nurseries, and family ministries.

A deep-seated sense of entitlement and specialness accompanied the boomers' ascent into adulthood. We were incorrigible and obnoxious (even when we were right) as we grew our hair long, protested the war, pushed the limits on controlled substances, fought valiantly in the sexual revolution, sought liberation (women's and otherwise), pushed for civil rights, and rejected the establishment, man! We were cool, boss, bad as we booked, got bummed out and stoned. It was tough to hang loose and just rap when our parents were such a drag, and things got heavy when the pigs harshed our buzz.[1] We were promised that we could have everything our parents had—and more. College became available to more and more young people, and a vision for the good life emerged, grounded in material wealth, success, possessions, and power. During the ascendancy of the baby boom, the term *baby boom* was coined. As the concept was explored, psychologists and educators expanded it. If 1946–1964 comprised a generation, then the eighteen previous years and the eighteen subsequent years could form generations as well. Throughout the 1970s and into the 1980s, generational theory emerged as a way of better understanding groups of people. The shared life experience of a group born within a generation, it was believed, could help predict values, beliefs, and behaviors. Educators and psychologists soon found out that the whole theory was deeply flawed, but pop culture, especially Madison Avenue, jumped on generational theory with both feet and exploited it for all it was worth.

Children born during the baby boom did indeed live through deeply formative experiences. As they came of age, television—perhaps the most influential invention of the twentieth century—reshaped culture. They grew up to witness the assassinations of two Kennedys and Martin Luther King, Jr., the war in Vietnam, the first moonwalk, and Watergate (and Richard Nixon's subsequent resignation). For American youth, these things were revolutionary and world changing. Before them, the last generation to experience such monumental events was the GI Generation (1908–1926), born during one world war to live through the Great Depression into a second world war. The technological advancements in electricity, plumbing, communications, medicine, and travel meant that a child born in 1908 or shortly thereafter was living in a world almost completely different from the one in which his or her parents grew up. But what about the generations around and in between the GI and the baby boom? The Lost Generation (1889–1907) lived through a minor depression, but their most memorable cultural shifts were mainly in art (art deco), literature (Wharton, Fitzgerald, Wodehouse), and music (the Jazz Age and the flapper era). Young people were viewed as slothful, fun-loving, irresponsible, and self-indulgent. It took the First World War to wake everyone up and set people on a more noble path. Many generational theorists—after studying the first generation of the twentieth century—simply decided to ignore it.

The generation between the GI Generation and the baby boom (1927–1945) was more interesting—after all, its members were still alive, and most of them were the primary authors and students creating generational theory—but no easier to pin down than the Lost Generation. Most were too young to fight in the war, but they were raised on radio, and they followed the war through radio shows and newsreels at the movies. They were the last generation of which less than 10 percent would go on to college, but they were the first generation to enjoy the benefits of drive-in movies (make-out pits), supermarkets (hangouts), drive-in fast-food restaurants, and pomade (most guys working on ducktails and James Dean spit curls). Dungarees and T-shirts shifted from the wardrobes of the poor kids on the edge of town to the cool kids from the newly emerging burbs. Smoking became the hip thing to do, and teenagers spent more time in cars than any previous generation or age group. Beyond the McCarthy hearings, the coining of the term *juvenile delinquency*, and the blossoming of the art form known as the B-movie, not a whole lot of culturally defining moments occurred. Most generational theorists settled on the Silent Generation as the label for this group, though later attempts were made to redeem the name, first as Builders, then as the Postwar Generation.

If Silent wasn't insulting enough, the generation born following the boomers (1965–1983) got slapped with baby bust, the Buster Generation, the Slacker Generation, Generation X (I prefer Gen X 'cause it sounds coolest), and even the 13th Generation.[2] Birth rates dropped precipitously early in the 1970s, and virtually nothing earth-shaking happened in the formative years of Gen X's maturation. Some of the more memorable cultural events for Gen X are the O. J. Simpson trial, Tonya Harding-Nancy Kerrigan skating fiasco, Lorena Bobbitt's "prank," Long Island Lolita Amy Fisher, the suicide of Kurt Cobain, the Teenage Mutant Ninja Turtles, *Star Wars* (movie, not missile project), Rodney King, and the Oklahoma City bombing.[3] One Gen Xer, earning the slacker name, summed up his generation thusly: "If it was on the news, I don't know it. . . . I don't watch the news."

Subsequent study indicates, far from being apathetic slackers, this generation may provide us with some of the deepest thinkers, most innovative philosophers and artists, and best global systems thinkers the world has ever known.

Now, all attention is shifting to the Millennial Generation (1984–2002).[4] A miniboom (actually larger numerically than the baby boom) that will once more rage through the world like a jug-gernaut—radically reshaping art, music, literature, theater, movies, the Internet, education, and so on to serve its own needs and match its own tastes—and cause generational theorists to salivate and shake. Projections about this generation are all over the map—they are more traditional, less traditional; like more structure, like less structure; have stronger ethical values, have looser ethical values; are more accepting of difference, are less accepting of difference; embrace change, reject change—more/less than every generation before them. In other words, we have no idea what our five-year-olds are going to want in twenty years, and everything we projected about children born twenty years ago has proved to be wrong or, at the very least, incomplete.

There is a fairly simple explanation: generational theory is grossly inadequate and fundamentally flawed. Although baby boomers had a deep central core of shared experiences that defined taste, preference, and expectations, that generation was an aberration. The diversity and complexity of our social structure make generational theory fall apart quickly. First of all, eighteen years is too long a span. There is virtually nothing similar in tastes, preferences, or desires between an average nine-year-old and an average nineteen-year-old. Second, when you add in contextual considerations—economic, educational, racial, geographic, ethnic, gender, and family—everything gets fuzzy. There is substantial evidence that baby boomers shared similar tastes in food, music, television programs, books, movies, and clothing. There is virtually no evidence that supports such claims for subsequent generations. Certainly, these generations consume what is produced for them, but producers are much quicker to respond to feedback and offer alternative choices. In 1965, you could find TV shows that 30 million people watched; but now, with the overall population double what it was then, a show is lucky to be able to bring in 10 million viewers. Music styles and categories have exploded, and no one style dominates the market as in the 1960s and before. Eclecticism is the order of the day, and our younger cultures are driving it, not reacting to it.

Churches are scrambling to apply generational theory in effective, meaningful ways, and for the most part they are failing. It's not their fault, however, but the limitations of generational theory itself. Trying to develop new worship styles that capture the interest of Gen X or the Millennials is a fool's errand. There isn't one style to find. Anything a church adopts to meet the needs of a generation will appeal to some, turn others off, and have no interest to still others. Generational demographics will not fit into neat, tidy, easily labeled packages. In fact, almost everyone but baby boomers despises labels.

The more helpful and accurate theoretical frame for churches to use is what I call phase of life theory. It holds that similar age groups share experiences and thoughts, and try new behaviors as they grow and mature. In this theory, we need to understand the life experiences that people face at various stages.

For example, young children are learning all the time, and they have limitless questions. Treating them like little adults won't help them learn and, in fact, may turn them off altogether. Older, preadolescent children are flexing their muscles, wanting to try adult things, as they figure out what they like and are good at. Early teens need to test limits, question authority, and cope with lifelong self-esteem issues. Older teens are beginning to move from concrete to abstract thinking. They are protophilosophers who are desperate to be independent and treated like adults. Postteens split quickly into two distinct groups—single adults entering work life and "the real world," and those pursuing higher education. Within these two spheres, further splits occur—those who stay single / those who mate or marry; those who have children / those who remain childless; those who stay together / those who split—but they have in common life decisions, such as choosing a career and lifestyle, renting or purchasing a first home, settling in or traveling, and so on. Good evidence exists that those who marry and have children are most likely to settle, and part of that settling is finding a church home. In midlife, attention shifts to finances, getting younger family members through school and launched while tending to older family needs, preparing for retirement, and dealing with a wide variety of health and wellness issues. In later life, health and wellness take center stage, along with making sure needs are cared for and, in many cases, worthy legacies are left for loved ones.

Many characteristics of phase of life transcend any generational designation. Teenagers were testing limits, questioning authority, adopting new technologies and trends, rebelling, and thinking about the big issues of life in the 1930s and 1950s and 1980s, just as they do today. Some concerns and interests of a couple having their first child today are precisely the same as those of their parents and grandparents in prior times. Conversely, the worldviews of two members of the same generation—one a single woman with a high-paying job that takes her around the globe, the other a married woman with two children living in a suburban community—may have virtually nothing in common.

Generational theory is fascinating. It raises truly interesting questions, but on careful examination, it explains virtually nothing. It fails the test of falsifiability. If you don't believe me, sit down with a room full of twentysomethings and attempt to find a simple descriptive statement that they will all agree is true and valid and accurate. You won't leave the room until the next generation has been born.

Instead, spend time trying to better understand the guiding concerns, issues, and values of people at different phases and stages through the life cycle.[5] Such knowledge transcends generational shifts and prepares people to better navigate the many changes and challenges that they encounter as they age (and, one hopes, mature).

It won't be long until the baby boomers age and expire (in the grand scheme of things). Our world will be changed for our time here, as it is with the passing of each new generation. But while the technologies change, and our methods and means evolve, the key life issues remain fairly stable: why are we here, what can we do, what can we become, and how can we find satisfaction and fulfillment? Churches that can help people confront and explore these questions will always have something of value to offer.

Notes

1. This is just a reminder about why our parents thought all of us might have been replaced by aliens, and a reality check on those of us today who cannot understand where our kids are coming from. Dig it? Right on.
2. Two men who jumped on the generational theory bandwagon and rode it for all it was worth are William Strauss and Neil Howe, who delineate generations from the very beginning of United States history through today (thus, the baby boom generation was number 12, the generation following, number 13). *Generations* (New York: Harper Perennial, 1992) and *The Fourth Turning* (New York: Broadway, 1996) are actually the very best books I have found on generational theory, both for what they say and for how well they expose the weaknesses of generational theory.
3. These are things that most Gen Xers remember. In a quiz given in different settings to groups born between 1965 and 1983, the things least remembered by participants were Vince Foster's suicide, Tiananmen Square, the end of apartheid, the election of Nelson Mandela, the first World Trade Center bombing, the Unabomber, and Jeffrey Dahmer.
4. Or the Mosaic Generation if you want to follow the evangelical churches' attempt to describe the multicultural makeup of this group.
5. One of the best books I have ever read on this subject is *Developmental Theories through the Life Cycle*, edited by Sonia G. Austrian (New York: Columbia University Press, 2008).

CHAPTER 3

POSTMODERNISM

THE DAY AFTER TOMORROW YESTERDAY

Americans have a bad habit of taking specific, technical terms and ideas and co-opting them for use in a common vernacular. One such term is *postmodern*. Originally coined in the late 1940s to critique architecture, it quickly blossomed into a complex philosophical construct to analyze and criticize art, literature, theater, film, politics, education, and a host of cultural and intellectual institutions. The fundamental premise of postmodernism is that the structures, rules, protocols, standards, and expressions of the modern era—from the dawn of the Industrial Revolution through, well, today (since many thinkers believe that we are still living in the modern era)—were limiting, narrow, erroneous, and, in many cases, destructive. Postmodernism is a refutation that the answers of modernity are universal—and an assertion that there are no absolutes, but that everything is merely interpretation. In the modern era, science displaced God, promising to cure all of humanity's ills. Postmodernists point out that science has not become our savior, and often the solutions of science create more problems. Modernity looked to the order and hierarchy of business and government to create a Utopian world. The failures of the world wars and the Great Depression led many to question this dream, and the later disgraces of the Vietnam War, Watergate, and Enron caused many more to reject the modern project's promises altogether. Modernity created narrative and artistic forms where authors and artists communicated personal messages. Postmodernism rejected the intentions of the artist in favor of the interpretation of the viewer. Modernity claims that the world is an orderly, secure, and comprehensible place governed by natural laws; postmodernism embraces chaos, serendipity, and mystery as the only absolutes.

But postmodernism is more than just living the questions and rejecting law and order. Postmodernism as philosophy is a way of better understanding the world and living with integrity in the swirl of ambiguity. Contemporary American culture has latched onto bits and pieces of postmodernism, turning it from a complex and integrated philosophical construct into an eclectic mess of jargon, myths, and misconceptions. No longer a positive means of creation, postmodernism (idiotically nicknamed PoMo in the dippy language of the day) is all about deconstruction, skepticism, cynicism, and rebellion; it's about breaking rules, distrusting order and hierarchy, being nonlinear,[1] embracing chaos, and rejecting institutions. Its primary adherents fail to realize, however, that these attitudes are not *post* anything. These thoughts and feelings are fairly eternal, emerging in every generation to challenge the status quo, to question entrenched thinking, and to confront injustice and ignorance. Many rubrics of the self-proclaimed postmodern are nothing more than evolved forms of modernity—modern dance, abstract art, concept architecture, avant-garde literature and poetry, punk music, communal living, quantum mechanics, and so on, and so on—and are a fairly good indication that we have not yet left the modern era (let alone moved to post-postmodernism, remodernism, neomodernism, PoMoGlobalism) but are still deeply entrenched in the modern world.

Whereas moderns threw off the shackles of a premodern world, postmodernists lovingly cart all the baggage that modernism provides—medicine, technology, art forms, and so forth. There are few, if any, truly postmodern advances and inventions. It is impossible to look at a crusader decked out in designer jeans with an iPod plug in her ears, texting her buddy on her cell phone, lugging her laptop in her backpack, which also holds the keys to her SUV, her bottled water, and her antidepressant prescription, and not see the epitome of modernity, regardless of who she doesn't like, disagrees with, and blogs with.

The implications for the mainline church have been astonishing. Disenchanted, cynical, angry, and lazy thinking has assaulted traditional thinking and practices, and the malcontents are winning. Since the church is an institution, it must be bad. Since rituals and traditions are old and linear, they must be corrupt. Since churches follow hierarchical structures and have rules, they must be oppressive. Since much of the literature, music, and art of the church is old, it must be invalid. These are the suppositions of many postmoderns, and those inside the church flinch and cower. They do so because they understand that there is some measure of truth to all of the criticism. The church is rigid. The church is out of step with the times. The church holds contradictory and oppressive views. The church is not perfect. But this is the humorous incongruity with American postmodernism—it condemns anything that is not perfect while holding the core belief that nothing is ever perfect. The modern world rests on the belief that everything can be improved, that nothing is ever good enough, that the answers to our problems lie just beyond our reach. Pursuing perfection is part of the modern mindset. This pursuit took us to the moon, keeps improving and evolving communications and computing technologies, cures more and more diseases, and adds value to day-to-day living of millions of people. Certainly, it has a shadow side, and it allows haves to continuously get more than the have-nots. The modern project needs to be criticized, questioned, challenged, and transformed—this is the real gift and value of postmodern thinking. Unfortunately, critique intended to salvage and improve is not often the goal of postmodernists. Instead, shrill and hostile voices denigrate, accuse, condemn, castigate, and decry anything modern, judging it to be fundamentally bad, irredeemable, and unworthy to exist. Hence, postmodernism earns a reputation of being negative, hopeless, and hostile.

Postmoderns look at the church and feast upon 1,001 shortcomings and failings of organized religion. Christians are judgmental. Christians are ignorant. Christians are selfish. Churches are irrelevant. Church leaders are egotists. Church rituals are outdated. On and on roll the negative assessments—which are usually framed as absolutes by people who say there are no absolutes—which critics use to invalidate any good that churches might offer.

Winning arguments—deciding who's right and who's wrong, who's on the side of the angels and who has descended to the realm of the devils—is a conceit of modernity, yet it is central to the postmodern approach to religion in America. What came before 1980 or so is wrong; what is emerging today is right. This simplistic and silly worldview prevents us from reaping the great benefits that postmodernism really has to offer.

And the problem is not all on the postmodern side. One of the greatest gifts of the postmodern philosophy is the deconstruction of accepted norms and the application of critical thinking and multi-phasic interpretation to messages and symbols. Postmoderns ask the question of *everything:* "What's really going on here?" What a fantastic question to ask of church, Scripture, theology, Christology, practice, ritual, worldview, philosophy, and values. What a rich opportunity to grow in the depth of our knowledge and beliefs, to create a sustainable and adaptive theology that will help us stay relevant in an ever-changing world. But, no, many Christian believers find such thorough examination to be threatening and dangerous. For some, asking questions is a sign of doubt and is fundamentally sinful. To ask critical questions from an evolved modern perspective of primitive and premodern writings, practices, beliefs, worldviews, and theologies is unthinkable. We condemn those who suggest it as heretics.

It raises the question, *What are we afraid of?* Why should we hesitate to examine the core beliefs of our faith? Why shouldn't we seek to have the very best understanding of our Scriptures, history, and tradition? If our faith is truly strong, how could it be anything but good to bring to bear our God-given gifts of reason, intellect, knowledge, and wisdom on our religion? Postmodernism reminds us that we have nothing to fear from the most thorough and careful examination. It is only the modern mind that has to fear finding answers we may not like.

Ignorance is always the enemy of faith (notice that this is a decidedly modern statement). It is often what we don't know, what we think we know, or what we wrongly know that causes most of our problems. I have had occasion to meet with young pastors, longtime church members, and non-church-going Christians to study and read together a sampling of modernist and postmodernist philosophers. The results are always enlightening, and they suggest a model for further exploration.

When people actually encounter some of the best thinking of Michel Foucault, Jacques Derrida, Ludwig Wittgenstein, Jürgen Habermas, Ken Wilber, Jean-François Lyotard, and Jean Baudrillard, they have three basic reactions:

"You mean this is what they really say?"

"Why is this such a big deal?"

"I pretty much agree with this!"

Postmodernism has acquired two undeserved reputations: as the end-all, be-all answer to everything or as the bogeyman beastie threatening to destroy all we hold dear. It is neither totally positive nor totally negative. It has little power to either create or destroy. What it offers is a valuable set of lenses through which to examine our modern world.

Mainline Protestant churches have much to offer, but they are not above criticism and they have incredible room to improve. Left to our own devices, we may never find any motivation to change—to correct the problems and strengthen the weaknesses evident throughout the church. Only with the perspective of persons outside the church—those who think, reason, and believe differently than we do—will we see ourselves with enough objectivity to know where to begin. Hierarchies are not inherently good or bad, but once they become corrupt, the result is rarely good. The quest for absolute truth is part of human nature, but when people confuse opinion with truth and then seek to impose their opinion as truth on everyone else, violence is sure to come. When every human interaction is cast as a win/lose encounter, people will seek power and control rather than harmony and justice.

We really aren't *post* anything today. But we are dissatisfied with a definition of *normal* that feels so limiting, unjust, oppressive, and unfulfilling. We look to the institutions that promise meaning and purpose, and we wonder why they seem so shallow and unimportant. Most spiritually seeking people outside the church are deeply inspired and excited by the idea of a body of Christ moving through the world to spread love, peace, mercy, justice, forgiveness, patience, and grace. There is widespread hunger for communities of openness and acceptance that will equip people to live grace-filled lives and will teach them how to use their gifts to share the love of God with the world. Yet when these same people observe most established churches, they do not find this powerful vision. Postmodern? Not really. Just unimpressed.

Note

1. Many postmodern people proudly proclaim that they are nonlinear thinkers. Educators and psychologists remind us that very young children and persons with autism or schizophrenia are primary examples of nonlinear thinkers. Nonlinearity is a disorder, not a goal.

CHAPTER 4

CRITICS, CRITICS EVERYWHERE, BUT NOT A THOUGHT TO THINK

In every generation, atheists, agnostics, non-believers, and unbelievers rally their resources to take on organized religion—usually the Western religions—Islam, Judaism, and, especially, Christianity. Due to the breadth, height, length, and scope of what Christians believe, we make easy targets. In various forms, those outside the Christian faith launch attacks in four basic areas: intelligence, ethics, morality, and sanity (Christians are stupid, dishonest, hypocritical, or crazy). In its newest incarnation, the attack is being led by the likes of Sam Harris, Richard Dawkins, and Christopher Hitchens[1] and a cadre of dissidents calling themselves "brights"[2]—whose whole argument is predicated on the assumption that no Christian listening to them will apply critical thinking skills to what they say.

Sam Harris, a philosopher-journalist, crusades against the danger that religion poses to modern society. His claims—not all unfounded—are that religion is more destructive than it is beneficial, and that history is filled with atrocities perpetrated by holy men and women (mostly men) in the name of their God or creed. Fair enough, so far, but the claim that religion causes fundamentally neutral human beings to do terrible things is never proved in Harris's diatribes. Conveniently, the idea that power-hungry, corrupt, and misguided people might corrupt religion to serve less-than-holy ends is casually dismissed. Perhaps the most insightful implication in Harris's argument is that we don't deserve religion because we abuse it so horribly, but that isn't something Harris says. He merely claims that religion is bad in and of itself.

Christopher Hitchens agrees. Hitchens, an erudite political commentator, philosopher, and columnist, glibly accuses religion of being responsible for everything that is wrong in the world. Citing the Islamic fundamentalism at the heart of the terrorist attacks on 9/11 and working backward, Hitchens proclaims that history and literature will bear him out that religion poisons everything it touches. Hitchens is a funny and intelligent writer, which makes him seem more knowledgeable than he really is. He is crafty. Once he claims his love and devotion for history and literature, he treats both like cheap prostitutes, using and abusing them, then throwing them aside without paying them. He revises and edits, pulling bits and pieces of fact out of context to weave his argument, snatching at any event that supports his thesis, disregarding all that might refute it. His analysis holds together wonderfully for anyone who doesn't read widely or know much history. Otherwise it bogs down as an opportunistic rant. Hitchens and Harris capitalize on their contempt for things religious—particularly Christian—by aiming at the easy targets, harvesting the low-hanging fruit.

At the center of the atheist message is a laundry list of bad behaviors—abortion clinic bombings, gay bashing, creationism and intelligent design, the Spanish Inquisition, Hitler's Aryan race agenda, pedophile priests, prosperity gospel preachers—all things that shame and embarrass the vast majority of rational Christians as well. But the fact that these things merely exist is taken as proof positive that the Christian faith is bogus and bad. The argument goes, you don't need religion to be good, and wherever religion exists, bad things happen, so let's do away with religion (and the bad things will all go away?).

Harris and Hitchens can almost be excused for their position—they have found a way to catapult themselves from relative obscurity into the spotlight of a hot-topic controversy (good career moves for both). But Dawkins is different. He is a smart man with a scientific background that he refuses to employ in his crusade against religion. He wrote the scientific classics *The Selfish Gene* and *The Extended Phenotype,* and introduced the concept of memes.[3] Somewhere along the line, this truly scientific genius seems to have lost his mind. He is an unapologetic atheist who not only rejects religious belief but also gleefully and arrogantly attacks anyone who chooses to hold religious beliefs. The same mind that approaches science with the very best inductive and deductive reasoning skills possible, abandons good scientific method to draw wild conclusions based on highly suspect deductive logic. If any student presented a scientific argument to Dawkins as sloppy as he presents his case against religion, it isn't a stretch to believe that Dawkins would flunk him or her.

Apparently, Dawkins has tried to pray for things and didn't get them, has tried to read the Bible literally and found errors and contradictions, has attended religious services and felt nothing, has examined history and discovered atrocities committed by religious leaders, and has noticed that some (most? all?) Christians hold some irrational and downright silly beliefs; therefore, Christianity must be false. Conveniently, the behavior of a Christian who has demonstrated great charity, mercy, sacrifice, or service is explained by the mix of meat, chemicals, and electricity of the brain and has nothing to do with religion. Dawkins is clear that the concept of a benevolent older man with a flowing white beard in the sky is not scientifically possible, and that the metaphoric explanations of holy Scripture do not really exist. He makes a good case—against people who hold a deeply immature and unexamined faith. What Dawkins (and Hitchens and Harris, for that matter) denigrates and rejects is not what the vast majority of Christian adherents believe—regardless of the sensationalized caricatures repeatedly presented in the media.

Certainly, within the frame of modern Christianity we still have members who hold a mythic/magic understanding of Bible stories, who are more concerned with monitoring the morality of others than with embracing and incarnating the teachings and Spirit of Christ. There are some in the fringes who believe that holiness is best proved with force and violence, who believe that Jesus said, "An eye for an eye, a tooth for a tooth," and who believe that by praying hard enough, you can make the hurricane hit someone else's house instead of your own. But these are the exceptions, not the rule.

Christian believers are found across the whole wide spectrum of intellectual, ethical, and emotional maturity. There are those who live in an intellectually and spiritually enlightened state where healing, reconciliation, justice, peace, and hope are their driving values and practices, but the critics of organized religion summarily ignore them. They are also the people who don't have any interest in wasting time in senseless debate with articulate malcontents who wish to pick a fight and attack people's most deeply held values.

Therefore, the critics of religion have their way. They continue to point out all that is wrong, all that has ever been wrong, and all that will continue to be wrong with religion. Taking it a step farther, not only is religion bad, but it ruins everything else too.

Why is it so important to these folks to wage war with religion? Well, for one reason, religion is getting scarier all the time. It may well be that the majority of Christians, Jews, Muslims, and other religious proponents in developed countries are moderately enlightened and mature; but in vast populations of the globe, the predominant worldview is primitive and premodern (with strong belief in magic, supernatural power, and the support of angry, vengeful gods), and the desire is to win one for the big guy upstairs. In the day when the weapon of choice was a rock or a club, that was one thing, but now that a relatively primitive culture can lay hands on nuclear missiles, the whole dynamic changes.

For way too long religion has been about being right, not being good. The whole concept of interfaith dialogue and cooperation is modern, and many people do not like its implications. If what we believe is true, then what other people believe is false. Why, then, should we have anything to do with people who aren't as smart, holy, and wonderful as we are? What's in it for us?

Of all the compelling arguments of the "brights," this is the best: religious people have not acted upon the best teachings and wisdoms of their traditions when push comes to shove. Most people who hold tightly to a faith do not feel that they are fortunate—they think they are superior. Much interfaith interaction is held not in an attitude of mutual respect and admiration but in patronizing tolerance.

There is no simple solution to this dilemma and the problems it poses for our high-tech global future. Religion is not now, nor has it ever been, separate from the social, political, economic, and educational realities of the dominant culture. The rare individuals who are deeply secure in their own faith are least threatened by the faiths of others, and they are instrumental in leading dialogue and discussion about ways to coexist peacefully and productively. Unfortunately, those people are not making the best-seller lists, sitting on Oprah's couch, reporting the evening news, or teaching at the premier colleges and universities. Oh, sure, they write, but who reads? They lecture, but who listens? They advocate and petition, but who responds? Religion is often defined by the lowest common denominators from the lunatic fringe. This leads to a polarization by the least enlightened on both sides. More than ever, the responsibility to create environments for loving, rational, respectful, and honest conversation falls to the women and men who lead local congregations. The best counterarguments to charges of stupidity, cupidity, arrogance, hypocrisy, and insanity are not said, but lived. If each local congregation commits to pursue a vision to be a force for good, things can begin to change. Will they change quickly enough to avert global disaster? No one can say. But we will be able to thank critics like Harris, Dawkins, and Hitchens for calling us to account . . . and perhaps shut them up once and for all.

Notes

1. Sam Harris, Richard Dawkins, and Christopher Hitchens have written *The End of Faith* (New York: W. W. Norton & Company, 2004), *The God Delusion* (Boston: Houghton-Mifflin, 2006), *God Is Not Great* (New York: Twelve Books, Hachette Book Group, 2007), respectively, but not overly respectfully.
2. Implying, of course, that religious believers are conversely dim, dull, weak, vague, lackluster, fuzzy, or mentally defective.

3. Memes (pronounced "meems") are units of cultural information similar to genes—units of genetic information—that pass from mind to mind, helping to create cultural awareness and evolution of thought. Memes explain how a collective unconscious might form and help describe ways that inventions and innovations spread quickly across great distances.

MINE IS BIGGER THAN YOURS

The word *growth* used to refer to development and maturity in the spiritual life, but in the twentieth century our focus shifted from quality to quantity. Size became a driving vision for the church. We have witnessed the birth and adolescence of the megachurch movement. Successful pastors model themselves after CEOs and entrepreneurial business leaders. Packing sanctuaries to bursting takes more of our time than carrying the good news into our community and world. The cult of personality and professionalism pervade our congregational settings, demanding an excellence of performance, preaching, and presentation.

Very few denominational and independent evangelical leaders see themselves in partnership. Rather than view all the many manifestations of Protestant Christianity as one body, most pastors regard themselves as being in competition with one another. The American landscape is a pie of limited proportions, and each congregation strives to take as large a slice as possible. The one with the most pew sitters wins.

There are both positive and negative elements in the competition culture we have developed in our Christian churches. On the positive side, we are motivated to be the best we can be. We want to provide a quality experience and meet the needs of the widest possible audience. Competition means we need to constantly strive to improve. On the negative side, however, our competition often turns to conflict, and the face we present to the world is one of discord, dissension, and disagreement. Part of our unspoken mission becomes to prove that our church is better than all the rest.

The gospel of culture says bigger is better. This is not our gospel. Our gospel says that the last shall be first, and the first shall be last. Our gospel says that together we are greater than the sum of our parts. Our gospel says that the church really isn't about us—it is about God and the need of God's healing for reconciliation and love. As long as we are referring to our church buildings, "mine is bigger than yours" is a negative sentiment. Perhaps one day soon, we will confess "my need to be forgiven is bigger than yours," and the road to Christian unity will be open to us all.

CHAPTER 5

MEGACHURCH MEGAMYTHS

The real gospel of twenty-first-century America is this: bigger is better. Whether you're talking about homes, cars, businesses, stores, fast-food meals (Supersize it!), computer memory, or churches, size matters. We love the *mega*, no matter where it may be found. Superstores abound, and the Wal-Marts, Home Depots, Best Buys, and Old Navys have forever changed what we're willing to accept. Size (big) connotes success (when referring to houses and SUVs), simplicity and savings (where we shop and eat), and our capacity to perform (in computers, for example). Added together, the megamentality is all about freedom and choices—having whatever we want, whenever we want it, wherever we want it. Digital cable television and the Internet are great examples of almost infinite choices customized to each individual preference and desire (TiVo, On Demand, and so on). We can access any information or entertainment at the touch of a button. We can remake the world to make ourselves happy.

It is no wonder that this attitude has found its way into the church. Churches exist—in many people's minds—to meet needs and give satisfaction. An enormous number of people subscribe to the Christian religion not as a way to serve others but as a way to receive comfort, support, encouragement, inspiration, and acceptance. The consumer mentality that pervades the larger American culture has become an insidious subset of Christianity in the United States. We demand that churches make us happy, and we can be happy only if we have many choices.

It has been bizarre to watch the evolution of big-church Christianity in America in the past forty years. I grew up in a large Presbyterian church in the Midwest. It was a bastion of brick and marble and glass (stained and clear), with adequate space for worship, learning, fellowship, and social services to the community. It had parking on three sides, was handicap-accessible, and even offered a smoker's corner in the memorial garden. Never in my wildest dreams did I see what was coming. A recent return visit introduced me to a completely different church. First of all, the building had expanded to occupy the entire lot of the former structure and parking. Shuttle buses run back and forth between the church and the parking lot three blocks away. Speakers in the buses blast contemporary praise music. Dropped off at the front door, members and visitors alike are welcomed by multiple greeters as they enter a mini-auditorium. Gone are the cross, candles, pews, carvings, and pipe organ of my childhood. Instead, theater-style seating faces a stage occupied by a rock and roll band and surrounded by three huge projection screens. Announcements, ads, and invitations scroll across the screens as music plays. For the first twenty minutes or so, the praise band performs music. While the congregation is invited to sing along, the performers enjoy displaying their talents by employing American Idol–like vocal gymnastics. Only the most adventurous worshipers even try to keep pace. The praise band worship leaders breathily offer prayers, and a small group dramatizes the story of Zacchaeus. A fiftysomething pastor in Izod shirt and khaki slacks, with a Madonna music video headset, jogs out to the front of the stage and delivers a seven-minute message on the importance of making sure Jesus can see you—his interpretation of the key point of the Lukan scripture. A closing song and an impassioned, "God rocks!" complete with fist pumping the air serve as our benediction. Immediately, the big screens begin hawking items from the gift shop, the coffee bar, the café, and the bookstore.

Long lines of people wait for the shuttle buses to return them to their cars, but an equal number divide into about a hundred small groups. This is a big church, drawing people from miles around, and worshipers tell me that they love it. Virtually no one is there from the days when I attended, but more than three thousand new faces worship in the church on a regular basis. What possible criticism could one have about a church that is reaching so many new people and gathering them together to worship God?

Well, here are a few less-than-positive views, and they are not limited to my old home church. I spent a few days talking to participants in a completely different (but similar) church to find out what it means to them to be a part of such a large, fun, exciting place.

First, I hung around the shuttle bus stop for a while following the service and asked very pointed questions about the church. Talking to more than a dozen people who had just attended the same service I did, I wanted to know what they thought was the main message from the service. Answers ranged from "Jesus loves us" to "God is awesome," but not one person referred to the Scripture or sermon (talk, message, whatever). I reframed my question to ask, "What did you learn about God this morning?" One man, speaking for many, scratched his head, scrunched his brow, and said, "You know, I don't remember anyone talking about God this morning."

Second, I asked a number of people what they did besides come to worship on Sunday. The vast majority said they did nothing else, but a few people confessed that they came to the coffeeshop, took guitar lessons, or attended an exercise class.

Then, I asked about small groups, learning, and Christian formation. One young woman said, "Oh, I think they have those, but you don't have to do them if you don't want to." Another woman chimed in, "The reason I like it here is that I can disappear. I'm just a face in the crowd, and everyone can just leave me alone."

Last, I asked what difference this church made in their lives. Some said it was fun, while others said it was really energetic and inspiring. A few said it was comfortable and didn't demand too much. I asked what it would mean to them if it closed its doors and disappeared. The response was unanimous—they'd go someplace else.

I spoke with many other people who were deeply committed to the church, found significant value in its ministries, and stated that they would miss it terribly if it went away. The church was not only their worship center but also an important part of their social network. All this is to say that there is as much positive about megachurches as negative. It is not my intention to attack the megachurch. My concern is that with great size come great headaches and some insurmountable problems that undermine the potential power and impact of Christian community.

A host of books and articles defend the megachurch and purport to answer unfair critics.[1] There are some truly silly complaints against large churches. Megachurches are inherently neither good nor bad, but as a congregation increases in size, the very definition of church changes. If the Christian life is best understood as a lifelong journey of learning, growing, serving, teaching, leading, and sharing—and if the biblical instruction and guidance are that this journey is best made in community—then it is important that people know, trust, respect, and value each other. The idea that the church is a center for commodity exchange where participants come to purchase and consume as individuals doesn't have much of a basis—in Scripture, history, or the Christian tradition. This is a uniquely modern, Western approach. Religious leaders who package Christianity and church as a product to satisfy the fickle desires of a consumer culture are not doing God any favors. Additionally, they reinforce a gross misunderstanding of what it means to be a Christian disciple. Discipleship is not, cannot be, a solo journey; it requires a community. The church is not a spiritual Wal-Mart where individuals come to shop for meaning, comfort, purpose, or forgiveness. The church is not a McDonald's where soul-hungry customers pick and choose from a value menu to fill up on Jesus junk food. Nor is the church like digital cable where the viewer flips through the channels until she finds something she's interested in. All of these allegories are inadequate for the environment where men and women wrestle with the biggest issues of life, death, truth, and meaning.

Leaders in many of the larger churches share problems of a different sort.[2] Most confess that they have no idea about the majority of the people who attend the church. They don't know names, stories, needs, or backgrounds. They hire associates and assistants and staff members to deal with the people. Many pastors of large churches have time for only three things—to preach, to travel and speak, and to make the CEO-style decisions needed to keep the church moving in a positive direction. Not only do many of these pastors feel out of touch with the majority of their members and visitors, but many also lament that they no longer have time for prayer, the study of Scripture, meditation, or personal development. Time once given to church fellowship events and visitation is now consumed by lawyers, accountants, media consultants, publishers, image specialists, and production directors and technicians. Some prominent pastors have guest appearances and speaking engagements booked clear into the middle of the next decade. In some rare cases, the senior pastors have become so important to the ongoing success of a particular church that life insurance policies have been taken out as financial protection.

One of the most pernicious rumors surrounding the megachurch is that it is all surface and no real depth—that it provides nothing but the most facile and superficial spiritual instruction. The argument continues that megachurches have more in common with Starbucks and Burger King, where people stop by to pick up a few things they want, to "have it their way," without much consideration for what they might need. The reason this rumor hangs around is that it happens to be true. Oh, certainly many participants in megachurches have deep, transformative spiritual experiences, and they find all they need to deepen their relationship with Jesus Christ. But megachurches also draw and appeal to a consumeristic, casual, and coddled culture founded on customer service and a strong sense of entitlement. People attend church to get for themselves what the church has to offer, and to the occasional browser, a good show trumps a serious service hands down. Megachurch pastors have learned the value of entertainment, and for a great many, presentation is much more important than content.

There is an inevitable and unavoidable trade-off between size (quantity) and impact (quality). Many studies—particularly those done by Christian Schwarz of Natural Church Development fame and those of The United Methodist Church—compare participation levels, knowledge, understanding, and engagement of those who attend megachurches and those who attend lesser lights.[3] Careful analysis of a church's impact on the surrounding community, the denominational affiliation (if there is one), and global concerns yields consistent results: ten healthy congregations of 300 members make more of a positive impact on participants, community, denomination, and world than any single 3,000-member church. Note that I said "healthy." There are many dysfunctional smaller congregations—generally, supporters of the megachurch love to compare a healthy specimen from their sample against struggling examples of the mainline—but on a level playing field, small to mid-size congregations do qualitatively better than their gigantic counterparts. In fact, the only two areas where megachurches far outclass smaller churches are overhead costs (it is cheaper to run one facility/campus, staff, and program than it is to run ten) and debt load.

Many of the strongest supporters of the megachurch make their arguments based on the testimonies of megachurch leaders and key participants. It is only natural that people who are responsible for the church would be positive. What about people who choose to leave megachurches? One research project specifically interviewed former members of a wide variety of large churches and megachurches about why they left. While these few statements reflect personal opinions, they also represent common, widely shared views.

> "It was exciting, and energetic, and even inspiring, but it was also insipid and simplistic and reductionist."

> "A little 'me-and-my-buddy-Jesus' goes a long way. What seemed so wonderful at the beginning got old really fast."

> "I attended for almost six years. I was part of a small group, and attended Bible study, and went to worship almost every week.

One day I woke up and realized, I didn't know God any better than when I first started going. I needed more."

"They wore me out. There was always a lot going on, but it was never clear what it was all for. Do you remember the movie *The Stepford Wives?* It was a lot like that."

"This may sound silly, but I got tired of meeting people at work or at friends' houses and finding out they went to my church and I had never seen them before. I got to the place where I wanted to know people and really be known by them. That was impossible for me in a huge church."[4]

This is not an either/or issue. Many debates over whether megachurches are good or bad are misguided. There is obviously a place for megachurches—many people prefer them, and a wealth of evidence indicates that thousands of people feel that a megachurch is helping them be faithful disciples. But perhaps we are close to a saturation point with these mammoth congregations. When Christian men and women who do not attend church are asked what kind of church might attract them, they overwhelmingly state that they would prefer a small, intimate, and deeply engaged congregation. Most will say that they want to *know* the people they are talking to and learning with in a significant way. But size is not the only issue. If size were the determinant issue, people would have plenty to choose from, since about 85 percent of mainline and evangelical Protestant churches have fewer than one hundred members/participants. People really want *healthy* small churches, and these are harder to find. People want safe, respectful, open, and tolerant environments. They want inclusive and diverse settings that are not rife with conflict, tension, and gossip. They want balance between personal development and meaningful service. They want to integrate acts of spiritual devotion with acts of mercy and compassion. They want to work, play, study, pray, eat, fast, and share with others who become true family and friends.

A former associate pastor of a huge southern congregation took me to lunch to talk about the future of the church. He read a book I had written, and he accused me—tongue in cheek—of ruining his ministry.[5] The idea that caught his attention was that most of the healthiest churches in my study shared the metaphor of becoming the body of Christ. He began to wrestle with the image, asking, "How large can a body expand before it becomes unsustainable?" He realized that once a church gets too big, the goal of being the body of Christ becomes impossible. He suggested to the other leaders of his church that perhaps they should divide the congregation into a dozen smaller, discrete satellite churches. No one was interested.

What is the church? What is it for? Is it a building, an organization, or an institution, or is it a people of God, empowered and equipped to be the hands and heart and voice of Christ for the world? Is the church the place where we go to worship and learn about God, or is the place we go to worship and learn about God where we are transformed from individual Christian believers into the church? Is the fact that a church is *popular* any kind of reliable indicator that it is *effective*? Regardless of a church's size, shape, or style, these important questions help us figure out why we're here and what God wants us to do.

Notes

1. One such book is *Beyond Megachurch Myths* by Scott Thumma and Dave Travis (San Francisco: Jossey-Bass, 2007). The authors describe much that is good about megachurches, but they are generic advantages that are true of most healthy churches regardless of size. There are many issues to celebrate

in the megachurch phenomenon, but it is irresponsible to ignore some of the major shortcomings.

2. Not all of these leaders identify these issues as problems. Most successful megachurch pastors have made peace with the trade-offs that gargantuism requires.

3. See Natural Church Development website, www.ncd-international.org, for a full description.

4. The General Board of Discipleship of The United Methodist Church, "Seeker Study," 2004–2007.

5. See Dan R. Dick, *Vital Signs: A Pathway to Congregational Wholeness* (Nashville: Discipleship Resources, 2007).

CHAPTER 6

THE PASTOR

DIRECT LINE TO THE MAN (PERSON) UPSTAIRS

At a new congregational development conference in Boston, I told a gathering of young pastors that they were an endangered species. Laity, I said, were awakening to the fact that the church was about them, was for them, and at its very best was them. The pastors in the room were outraged.

"There is no church without us!" one young man exclaimed.

"You're demeaning the calling of ordained clergy," chimed in another.

"You're full of s**t!" summarized a third.

Let it suffice to say, these novice clergy leaders were less than thrilled with the idea that they might be irrelevant. That, of course, is too harsh. I never said that pastors were irrelevant. I merely commented on the reality of an empowered, educated, and motivated laity that wanted to be the church in the world. It's fascinating that so many pastors found that threatening instead of encouraging.

Even in our supposedly enlightened and emerging era, pastoral leaders like to be in charge. Clergy leaders of today deeply desire the unquestioned hegemony of bygone days. The success of autocratic command-and-control CEOs in our largest churches perpetuates the myth that pastors are in charge of the church. Pastors are servants and shepherds when they do their job well, but a large population of our clergy leaders finds such a role insulting and disrespectful. While many ordained ministers pay lip service to the empowerment of the laity, few truly believe in it or seek to make it happen.

What is the role of an ordained clergyperson in a healthy, thriving faith community? The answer to this question is less than clear. Some feel that the pastor is the incarnate presence of Jesus in the midst of the congregation. Ordination confers (in their opinion) absolute authority, and many clergy leaders believe that they are irreplaceable. In many of the healthiest congregations, it is actually almost impossible to identify the pastor; laity and clergy share equally in the ministry. All too often, though, ordained ministers get confused, believing themselves, instead of Christ, to be the head of the body.

Although many ordained leaders would like to be the final authority in all things congregational, there are only three roles that they can fill better than the majority of laity leaders: (1) resident theologian, (2) administrator of the sacraments, and (3) shepherd and guide to spiritual pilgrims on their journey of faith.

Ordained clergy hold a unique position in a congregation to preach and to teach—though they do not have an exclusive right to either. It is absolutely reasonable to expect our ministerial leaders to study Scripture, understand theology, interpret and translate original biblical languages, be knowledgeable about church and Christian history, and be well acquainted with the major beliefs of world religions. Having these understandings prepares clergy leaders to truly teach and offer real value as people explore the deepest questions of life and faith. Ordained leaders should devote a significant amount of time and energy to continuously develop and expand their knowledge in these areas. Others might study and learn much, but ongoing learning is central to the pastor's role in the life of a growing congregation.

While the actual performance of sacraments in mainline Protestant denominations is simple—saying a few words, consecrating a few elements, dipping, dripping, breaking, sharing—they are also deeply symbolic and substitutionary. Ordained clergy take vows to faithfully adhere to rituals, principles, and practices of the faith, and to administer the sacraments on behalf of the community of faith. Men and women make serious commitments to offer these historic and fundamental graces in the name of Christ. Many make the case that anyone can offer the Eucharist or baptize a child or adult, but this practice disconnects the act from Christian tradition, the historic cloud of witnesses, and the transcendent communion of the saints. Ordained clergy are set apart to serve, and one of the most valuable acts of their service is to administer the sacraments.

Clergy leaders are spiritual guides who commit their lives to shepherd and guide others. The word *pastor* actually means "shepherd." Men and women gather together as the church to learn what it means to follow Christ and live authentic lives of faithful discipleship. Pastors act as mentors, coaches, trainers, teachers, and models for spiritual development. They oversee the whole community, working to knit and unite the various gifts, passions, skills, and abilities of individual members to build and strengthen relationships. Effective and conscientious pastoral leaders always look to the welfare of the group over the demands of individuals. Clergy are ordained to do all in their power to build the body of Christ every-where they serve.

In any setting, these three functions are more than a full-time job. Yet many pastoral leaders feel that these functions are inadequate or unfulfilling. They seek respect, admiration, power, control, and authority. They enjoy being in charge, and they reject any and all attempts by others to question their leadership. In many locations, laity members share this view, seeing their pastor as the person who runs their church.

Throughout the nineteenth and twentieth centuries, ordained ministry evolved from spiritual calling into accredited profession. As the role and function of the pastoral leader evolved toward professionalism, many clergy leaders clung desperately to the image of priest as monarch, king (or queen) of the puppet kingdom of the congregation. By the divine right of kings, pastors settled into the throne.[1] The failing of this metaphor is its assumption that the opposite of monarchy is anarchy—if one is not in charge, then no one is in charge. Chaos, confusion, darkness, sin, and suffering are certain to ensue. It is impossible for many ordained clergy leaders to believe that laity will create anything short of hell on earth if they are given too much responsibility for their own salvation. The line of reasoning goes—people need Christ, the church is Christ's agent in the world, and I am the leader of a congregation of the church; therefore, people need me. Without me, nothing good can happen.

This appears to be an unexamined philosophy that carries over from an earlier time. Just a few decades ago, ordained clergy leaders were among the most educated members of the American culture. They certainly were some of the best read, widely traveled, adequately trained, and most articulate civic leaders. This distinction is no longer true. Many participants in our congregations hold multiple graduate degrees.[2] Many of our laity can preach and teach circles around the majority of our ordained pastors. Clergy leaders no longer travel more than the average person. Today's clergy are no longer the cream of the crop, but more likely just part of the herd (to mix a metaphor). It is not that clergy are not special, important, or valuable—it is just that they are not as special, important, or valuable as they like to believe.

I am an ordained United Methodist pastor. I feel honored, privileged, and humbled by my ordination and consecration. I take very seriously the vows I have made and the solemn duties with which I have been entrusted. But I also know that many gracious and blessed men and women, who have as much to offer to Christ's church, have not taken the same road as I. I am proud to call them friends and colleagues, and I would never question whether their call and ministry were somehow inferior to my own. Empowered and gifted laity are not my competition but my partners.

Ordained clergy do not have a direct line to God, nor do they possess rights, privileges, and benefits withheld from the hoi polloi. Though many clergy leaders confess that they feel like an endangered species, they also admit that they are not always clear about their roles and responsibilities. Pastors in first appointments and assignments are often startled, frustrated, and disillusioned by the expectations they encounter when they begin their ministry. Numerous clergy leaders come to ministry with a very specific sense of calling and service, but the reality of leading a congregation often buries that vision and worldly demands pull them in completely different directions. Going to committee meetings, overseeing finance campaigns, negotiating copier contracts, monitoring custodial duties, and mediating skirmishes between the organist and the choir director expand to completely eradicate the grandest plan for evangelizing the city and saving the world. Before long, the busyness of running the church displaces the business of being the church.

Modern congregational leaders set aside more time to read business books than to read theology. They spend between five and twelve times as much time each day on the phone as they do in prayer. On the average, they give two hours each week to Bible reading, while during the same week they spend seven hours on the Internet.[3] The questions may fairly be raised, How deep is the well from which modern-day clergy leaders are drawing? Where do they renew, restore, and retreat? How do they feed their souls, discern their vision, and plan for the future? There are no simple answers to these questions, and none of them may be answered in a vacuum. The challenges of leading a faith community are enormous—much too large for any one individual. It was never God's intention—at least according to the four Gospels—that one set-apart, specialized leader would take the task on himself or herself. At the very least, the model is two by two, but a team of twelve is probably more reasonable. Even the Pauline Epistles, where hierarchical congregational models first appear, are very clear that congregations are led by networks of gifted individuals. Pastors—ordained and otherwise—are gifted just like everyone else, interdependent members of the body of Christ. Christ is the head of the body; clergy and laity—ministers all—are the hands, feet, heart, and voice.

The most exciting and vibrant churches are those where the whole congregation is engaged in spiritual formation and meaningful service. In such congregations, everyone teaches and everyone learns. Everyone leads and everyone follows. Everyone gives and everyone receives. And in the best of the best, pastors dedicate themselves to making sure it all runs smoothly. Pastors continue to serve an important role in the life of the church—a role they were always meant to play—as "servants of Christ and stewards of God's mysteries" (1 Cor 4:1), alongside all those seeking to become disciples of Jesus Christ.

Notes

1. It is enlightening to look at church furnishings from the 1800s and 1900s. Often, the preacher's chair in the sanctuary or chapel very closely resembled a throne. Once reserved for the King of kings (and never occupied by a human being), these chairs were claimed by the pastor-in-charge, further conveying the message that he (or in rare cases, she) was standing in for Jesus.
2. Though clergy attempted to keep pace with their own version of doctorate level degrees. Having pursued both a PhD and a Doctor of Ministry degree, I can readily confess that the DMin demanded neither the rigor nor the sacrifice of a PhD.
3. Dan R. Dick, "Clergy Health and Wellness Time Usage Study," General Board of Discipleship of The United Methodist Church, 2002–2003.

How Low Can You Go?

(Expectations, That Is)

Ben and Terry were (probably still are) delightful people. Both professionals with lots of energy and enthusiasm, knowledge-able, friendly, happy—just the kind of young people any church would love to have as members. That was why they couldn't figure out why I wouldn't let them join the last church I served. The Wantage United Methodist Church, sad to say, had standards, and anyone wishing to join the church had to attend a thirteen-session new-member orientation class. Ben and Terry thought the require-ment was ridiculous. The idea that they should have to meet any kind of requirement insulted them. Imagine, then, how much angrier they were three years later when they came to me, wanting to have their baby "done," and I refused to baptize him unless they were serious about becoming active participants in the life of the congregation. I attempted to walk them through the baptismal ser-vice to help them understand the vows they were making to God and their child, as well as comprehend the covenant that the congregation would make to be a part of their child's life. It didn't take. They found a church a couple miles away that would sprinkle their darling with no cost—monetary, emotional, or spiritual.

I have shared this story with many pastors over the years, and I am constantly amazed at the large number who tell me I was way out of line. "It's not up to us to withhold the grace of God," they say, or "We shouldn't make it any harder on people to get to heaven than it already is," or "Membership classes are a complete waste of time—people don't remember anything from them anyway." When I ask them to explain their theology of baptism or to define true membership in the community of faith, the response is generally blank stares. If there is no expectation that Christian believers have a responsibility to the larger congregation (with a reciprocal responsibility from the congregation to the Christian-in-formation), why even bother receiving them into membership?[1]

Congregations, by definition, are covenantal communities united and bound by core beliefs, values, shared practices, and goals. The process of spiritual formation and growth in Christian discipleship requires participants to engage in a variety of practices. There are widely shared beliefs that prayer, knowledge of Scripture, worship, fellowship, study, and service are essential components of Christian growth. Celebration of sacraments in community, fasting, meditation, and Sabbath keeping are also viewed as helpful, if not essential, experiences. Congregations exist to facilitate, promote, support, and teach these practices. Leaders in congregations have the sacred responsibility to hold accountable those who vow to live as Christian disciples, teachers, and servants to these practices. Without accountability, there cannot be true growth.

Yet the vast majority of Christian congregations ask some form of the following promise—"Will you uphold this congregation by your prayers, presence, gifts, and service, confess Jesus Christ as Lord, and do all in your power to avoid sin?"—with absolutely no process or intention to measure and evaluate performance. Each person who joins a church does so on his or her own terms. It is not unusual for people to make the solemn vow to support the church and then show up only for an occasional Christmas Eve service.

How have we become a church of such low expectations? There is no single, simple answer, but the few we have are a little depressing.

First, we live in a very individualistic society, where most people believe that no one else has the right to tell them to do anything. A relationship with God is a deeply personal thing, and in our modern culture, it has become a private thing as well. Americans rarely put the welfare of the group ahead of personal needs and desires.

Second, we live in a busy world, where every minute of our day is tightly scheduled and our downtime is filled with entertainment. We are distracted by many things—work, family, television, the Internet, school, friends, telephones, and on and on—and find little left over for spiritual disciplines and practice. It is all we can do most weeks just to shoehorn in an hour for church. And as leaders in the congregation, we have to pack as much into that hour as we can. No longer is worship about God; it is all about us. We don't have time to waste just worshiping (where the gathered people praise and honor and give thanks to God)—we've got to have worship *and* evangelism (let's use worship as a tool to attract new people!) or worship *and* stewardship (let's use worship as a crowning event in our stewardship campaign!) or worship *and* missions (let's use the worship hour to do a mission project travelogue!) or, best yet, worship *and* the arts (let's do a choir/orchestra/jazz/rock/liturgical dance/hand bell/drama show!). No wonder many people leave the church more tired than when they arrived.

Third, church isn't the part of our identity it once was. Church isn't who we are, but where we go once or twice a week. Many people do not consider joining the church as the launch of a lifelong journey; to them, it is a destination. Saying yes to joining a fellowship isn't a beginning, but an ending.

Fourth, clergy and laity leaders are too embarrassed to ask of newcomers what they themselves do not practice. The majority of Protestant pastors claim they are too busy, too pulled along by competing demands to pray, to worship, to study the Bible and read theology, or even to engage in service beyond the church they serve. When congregational leaders do not model disciplined behavior, their words carry little weight.

Fifth, we don't want to do anything that might keep people away from church. Numbers are way too important. If we require too much, people will stay home. Much better to demand next to nothing, avoid anything that might make a person feel guilty, and allow people to be Christian in whatever way is most comfortable to them. We cannot afford to waste time thinking about being honest, modeling integrity, or pleasing God here.

Sixth, most spiritual disciplines are not really much fun. Fasting is unpleasant. Prayer can become boring. The Bible is confusing. Worship requires us to get out of a comfy bed. Christian service requires sacrifice and may take us to people we would rather avoid. Sitting in a pew or chair for an hour or so each week is more than enough—we don't want to get carried away. The goal then becomes how to make the hour in the pew as enjoyable and painless as possible.

Welcome to the First Church of the Lowest Common Denominator. Everything is geared to keep people happy and content. Nothing challenges, disquiets, or discomforts. Everything is offered at the beginner level. Don't like creeds? Fine, they're gone. Banners are tacky. We'll replace them with screens and projectors. Passing of the Peace make you nervous? Outta here! Responsive Psalter readings? Too slow. A cross might offend someone or remind people that they're actually in a church. Can't have that. If we work hard enough, maybe we can convince people that they're actually watching us on TV instead of sitting in a *sanctuary* (which is such a stuffy word—we need to stop using it; *worship center* sounds much more acceptable).

Our deep desire not to offend anyone has resulted in a fascinating counteralienation. Thousands of Christians in America who are struggling to grow as disciples who have given up on the church— not because it demands too much, but because it demands so little. They are turned off by the superficial and pedestrian approach to religion. They seek challenge and discipline—looking for the same kind of drive and intense pressure that personal trainers demand of athletes, but in the spiritual arena. They desire help to stay focused and committed on the Christian journey. They want coaches who will teach them to pray, counsel them in ways to improve, measure their development, and hold them accountable to the goals they set. Many of these people cannot figure out why the demands in the church are so low when the stakes are so high.

Some churches employ membership standards, clear expectations, valid metrics, and fair accountability structures, but they are rare. Those that function best do not impose a set of standards from on high—the leaders of the congregation do not pass down a decree that "this is the way it's going to be!" Instead, members of the congregation most desiring a healthy, growing relationship with God gather together and hammer out reasonable expectations that everyone is willing to live with. From consensus emerges a covenant—a set of ground rules and expectations that are easy to understand, are fair, and that will help everyone grow together toward individual goals. This process of crafting a workable system for accountability is elegant and effective. It is much more difficult for persons to resist being held accountable to a standard they set for themselves.

The question always arises, "So, what do you do with the people who don't want to participate? Do you kick them out of the church?" Well, no, not physically. A congregation will always be open to welcome and care for anyone in need. But as far as being a full member of the covenantal community, each person has to make his or her own decision. If being a member of the community requires meeting a particular set of standards, then only those who do so get to be members. Those who fail to meet the standards don't get to be members. It is still up to each individual whether he or she wants to be part of the community, but the community, not each individual, sets the rules.

The message of most contemporary churches is that membership means absolutely nothing. There is no difference between members and nonmembers. People can join and do nothing; people can visit and receive exactly the same treatment. It is no wonder that people don't care about joining churches anymore. Some commentators claim it is a sign of the times—people just don't join clubs anymore[2] —but this begs the question when one sees the number of health club memberships, book clubs, online communities, and 101 smaller specialty groups. The form changes, but the functions stay pretty much the same. Membership in a group distinguishes the inside from the outside. It offers an aspect of identity that is special. People do not join a health club thinking they can pay their membership dues when and if they feel like it, can obey only the rules they agree with, and can treat the equipment any way they want to. People who think this way *can't be members*!

A United Methodist bishop heard me talk to a large group about membership standards and accountability. He said, "You cannot seriously tell people that it's OK to keep people out of the church. Accountability has to be tempered with grace—we can suggest that people practice spiritual disciplines, but we cannot demand it." As much as I respect this leader, I disagree with him completely. Jesus is reported to have had clear standards for discipleship, and while it saddened him, he did not let everyone who wanted to, call himself or herself a disciple.

As long as our driving values are members on the rolls and warm bodies in our pews, it is anathema to raise our expectations and hold people accountable. Attendance figures and dollars in the collection plate are simply way too important to us right now. We cannot—we will not—do anything to threaten our income and incoming. The world—and the real work of the church—can wait. It will still need redemption and transformation when we get around to it. My hope is, there will still be enough people who care.

Notes

1. Many churches have abandoned membership categories of any kind, preferring to refer to people as participants, attendees, or customers. The point isn't actually about membership but about what it means to be a part of a group, family, community, or congregation, and if it is fair and reasonable to expect certain standards of conduct, engagement, and commitment. The jury is still out on this one.
2. One great example is the fascinating book by Robert Putnam, *Bowling Alone: The Collapse and Revival of American Community* (New York: Simon & Schuster, 2000).

CHAPTER 8

CLONING PASTOR HAPPY

 His face (trust me, this is almost always a guy) smiles at you off the dust jacket of his latest best seller. He's smart, handsome, middle-aged-trying-to-look-younger, and he knows everything *you* need to know about God, church, leadership, success, Jesus, the Bible, self-help, and raking in money hand over fist. He pastors a megachurch, he appears in magazines and on TV talk and news shows, and he humbly proclaims, "It's not about me."

Who is this guy? Basically, he is the newest in a long line of celebrity pastors who becomes the poster child for all aspiring ministers hoping to scale the heights of ecclesial fame and fortune. The name of this person isn't important—a decade from now no one will remember it. What is important is that he represents the core values and vision of a significant number of Christian leaders in America.

Who wouldn't covet the notoriety of leading a huge ministry in a mammoth church with televised reach across the globe? Who wouldn't love having tens of thousands of people hanging on your every word? Who wouldn't love walking into any Barnes & Noble in the country and seeing a nicely retouched photo of himself smiling off a strategically placed floor display?

The name that comes to mind is Jesus, actually. Our Gospels give strong indication that Jesus himself struggled with the trappings of celebrity, and he fought mightily to help people stay focused on the message rather than the messenger. But then again, he didn't have a jumbotron.

Even lacking the clout of modern technology, Jesus kind of lost the battle with celebrity status. Repeatedly through history, the man Jesus has become an iconic figure, bumping the risen Christ from the limelight. As recently as Mel Gibson's *Passion of the Christ*, the suffering human Jesus takes center stage. Jesus becomes more important than his own message, teachings, and purpose. A central message of the emergent church movement is a get-to-know-Jesus pretense that emphasizes Jesus as buddy and pal more than incarnate spirit of the living God.

It is part of human nature to seek actual living, breathing models to emulate and pursue. It is much easier to be like someone else than it is to be like a concept or abstraction. Doing what Jesus did (up to a point) is easier than doing what he said. Knowing Jesus as my personal Lord and Savior allows me to set as my life's goal to be more like Jesus. I already know I can never be the Christ.

And so it goes in the modern era. "What would Jesus do?" gives way to "What would Joel do?" or "What would Pastor Rick do?" or "What would Bishop Jakes do?" This idea isn't all bad. People need models and mentors. Pastors stand in a unique position to challenge, inspire, invite, and encourage new thinking and good behaviors. A pastor with significant influence can be a great force for good . . . or a disaster waiting to happen (think Ted Haggard). The problem is not that human leaders are basically bad people—almost every Christian leader I have ever met believes in what he or she does and says and has the best intentions at heart—but that they are basically human. Human beings are flawed, and no amount of airbrushing is going to guarantee that they won't fall short at some point.

In my lifetime, only one high-profile celebrity religious leader maintained a pristine image from start to finish, and that was Billy Graham. I'm talking not about his message, but about his vision. I never got the sense that Billy Graham thought what he was doing was about him. Almost every other leader that I can name came across as an empire builder or as heir apparent to Jesus himself. Walking into stadium-seating sanctuaries past bronze statues of the pastor, watching twenty-foot-tall images of the preacher's head on big screens, and hearing endless personal anecdotes of piety and epiphany from well-dressed, finely coiffed, exquisitely shod, image-coached performers make me wonder whether we haven't, perhaps, lost focus.

And it doesn't stop with the megachurch megastars, either. These popular pious personalities are not the exception, but more the standard. Churches of all sizes, stripes, theologies, locations, and lifestyles experience many of the same leadership quirks. Recently, a church I know of held auditions for a preacher, wanting to make sure that a newly hired leader would look good on camera and sound good on radio. Applicants read from a prepared text—the church wasn't even concerned about the person's theology or ability to craft a coherent message!

A survey of recent trends in church staff hiring is illuminating. In the past decade, popular church staff positions include production coordinator, technical designer, sound and lighting tech, voice coach, media director, hair and makeup designer, and (my favorite) glamour coordinator. If church isn't becoming a show, and pastors and preachers aren't becoming celebrities, what are all these positions about?

It is not that churches should avoid broadcasting their services and reaching as large an audience as possible. That isn't the real problem. The problem emerges when Jesus Christ and the Christian gospel take a backseat to the performance. Churches have made decisions about key components of Christian worship based on broadcast schedules and set blocking rather than on the integrity of the experience. Crosses, candles, Bibles, and paraments are removed because they don't shoot well, and creeds, confessions, prayers, and offerings are dropped because they drag or cause the broadcast to run long. One church that holds its full service each week, then edits a one-hour broadcast afterward, uses a simple guideline in deciding what to eliminate and what to leave in: take out anything that might make people feel bad.

There is nothing wrong with personal stories, humor, emoting, or high drama in preaching. Good delivery can add impact and power to a decent message. But the cliché "moderation in all things" caught on because of its inherent wisdom. Too much of a good thing is not a good thing. Too many sermons today are well-scripted comedy routines, Lake Wobegon-esque reminiscences, manipulative heart-tuggers, or weepy/moaning confessions—not illuminations of the gospel message of Jesus Christ. In fact, words like *Jesus, God, sin, resurrection,* and *grace* are disappearing from many sermons altogether. At a national United Methodist conference I watched in amazement as a young woman preacher rehearsed her tearful message, receiving coaching from a man who called out helpful tips: "Let your voice break up more," "This is a good place to sob," and "Pull the crying back just a little so that people will understand your words." Somehow I can't see Jesus turning to Peter and saying, "So, is the turning over the tables thing too much, or should I, like, roar when I do it? I want to make sure we get there before noon so the light is on my good side."

Throughout the history of the Christian faith, there have been superstar personalities. Tales of camp meetings and revivals, Burt Lancaster as Elmer Gantry and Robert Duvall as Sonny Dewey in *The Apostle*, Billy Sunday and Aimee Semple McPherson come to mind. It is a normal and natural part of the evolution of any message-based movement. But these examples are aberrations, not aspirations. It is a sad commentary that such celebrity-style religious icons are lifted up as archetypes for effective pastoral leaders. It sets up a dynamic for frustration and failure for literally hundreds of otherwise gifted men and women who are answering a call to ministry and service. And yet denominational offices, judicatories, synods, and conventions continue to highlight the success stories of a few prominent individuals as exemplary. The implicit message is that everyone should aspire to be like Hybels or Warren or Osteen or Jakes.

Let me be clear. I am not criticizing the golden elite who have risen to the top of the heap. If they seek personal glory, well, then, I do have a problem with that, but for the most part, the celebrity clergy I know are decent, committed individuals who believe in the work they do. Being famous, having a large church, running a television ministry, and hosting leadership institutes are all fine, but they are going to be the domain of the chosen few. Most pastors can try as hard as they possibly can, and they never will come close to the style, performance, and results of a Joel Osteen or a Rick Warren—and they shouldn't have to.

Ultimately, church isn't about how good or popular or brilliant or successful the pastor is—or at least, it shouldn't be. Our culture loves to American Idolize anyone with the potential to be larger than life. We are drawn to the glamorous, the funny, the provocative, and the profane. A few capitalistic Christians have exploited this propensity for all it's worth, with some incredible results. That doesn't make it good, right, or preferable. There is little evidence that our world is a better place for these monolithic Christian meccas. No—lives are changed, hearts are transformed, and people join together to be the heart and hands and voice and eyes of Christ in communities of faith of all sizes, shapes, locations, and traditions, led by women and men of varying knowledge, skills, gifts, and styles. Where the focus is on loving God with heart, mind, soul, and strength and loving neighbor as self, the world is made a better place. God doesn't simply rely on suave, sophisticated, slick media personalities to bring heaven to earth. God uses whoever is willing, wherever possible, to bring light and life into the world.

Faithful and effective Christian leadership isn't measured by the size of the congregation, the reach of the broadcast ministry, the cost of the preacher's church, or the salary he or she can command. No one ever becomes a better minister by trying to be like someone else—that's not leading; that's following. Christian leaders succeed best when they are free to be themselves—to employ the gifts, skills, passions, and personality God gave them.

Any time a pastor implicitly (or explicitly) says, "Look at me!" there is a problem. We need fewer distractions from focusing on Jesus Christ, not more. We need selfless and humble people who step to the side, point our attention to God, and encourage us to become more like Christ. We need denominational and regional leaders who help us focus on a vision for the world, not who promote the performance of a few select men and women. We need to be reminded again and again that the church really isn't all about us, but it is about God and doing God's will.

CHAPTER 9

MORTGAGING THE MISSION

"The church is a business!" I hear this comment frequently. It is generally pronounced defensively to explain why so much of our time, energy, and effort is spent in fund-raising and financial planning. There is no argument that the organizational institution we call church is a business and needs to be run effectively, efficiently, honestly, and ethically. Administration is listed among the spiritual gifts that God bestows on the congregation to fulfill its mission and ministry. The better we run the organization, the more effectively we can succeed in our witness and service.

But the business of the church is not the purpose of the church. The administrative needs of a congregation are not its primary task; they support the primary tasks of reaching people in the name of Jesus Christ, relating them to God and a community of faith, helping them grow and mature in their faith, and equipping and empowering them to live their discipleship each and every day.

Admittedly, ministry takes money. Everything requires money these days, and the more money you have, the more you can do. However, much of the money we make isn't really used for ministry. It is questionable that much of the rising amount of church expenditure is actually necessary to the mission and ministry of the church. For example, some of the fastest growing areas of church spending are lighting, landscaping, paving, art, statuary, fountains, and electronic security. Certainly, these things reflect secular values and cultural expectations, but ministry?

An examination of spending trend lines in Protestant churches over the past one hundred years also raises questions. A positive trend line indicates an increase in spending, while flat and negative trend lines indicate stagnation or a decrease. The two trend lines that show the steepest increase are for money spent on salaries and buildings. Many pastors lament that the pay for clergy is poor—at least, not competitive with comparable professions and education levels—but with adjustments for inflation, pastors today make close to seven times as much as their predecessors of one century ago. Funding for buildings has increased even more—in many cases ten to thirty times as much is spent today as one hundred years ago.

The trend line on money spent on church programs has stayed essentially flat—we spend about the same percentage of budget today on Sunday school, Bible studies, fellowship groups, and resources that we did in the early 1900s. The main difference here is that we spend less on outreach than on caring for our members.

The only dramatically negative trend line is in the money spent on missions. On average, Protestant churches have decreased the percentage of mission spending from about 40 percent of total budget to a little less than 1.5 percent. For many churches, the only things that prevent the percentage from being zero are denominational obligations and emergency special offerings.

The overall trend of the past one hundred years is to spend more and more money on ourselves while spending considerably less on those outside the church. Good, bad, right, or wrong, this is a fairly accurate commentary on American values. Congregational leaders may claim that the reason we spend money on ourselves now is to allow us to do a better job spending money on others later, but all the evidence indicates that the more money we spend on ourselves now will enable us to spend more on ourselves in the future. Our fastest growing churches experience a perpetual cycle of building project after building project, capital campaign after capital campaign, and mortgage after mortgage.

This cycle of expansion and development cannot help impacting our sense of identity as church and the roles of our congregational leaders. One poll of large church pastors from a variety of denominations indicated that 20 percent of them still identify their primary role as prophet, preacher, or spiritual guide, but more than 65 percent of them claim CEO as the most appropriate representation and description of their function in the church. It is not unusual to hear such pastors say things like, "I serve as a tenth trustee," or "My job is to run the company," or "I spend more time reading municipal codes and insurance forms than I do the Bible."

One of the historic ordination questions in the Methodist tradition is, "Are you in debt so as to embarrass you in your work?" For John Wesley, the definition of *embarrassing debt* was the equivalent of two weeks' wages, but we won't go there. Instead, I wonder how this question would be answered if it were posed to the leaders and trustees of our local churches. Many churches in the United States are carrying exorbitant debt loads—as much as seven times their annual revenue. To pay off this debt, and to cover the interest it incurs, many churches have reduced money designated for missions, outreach, and program. Many churches create endowments, not for missional growth and development, but as a hedge against future debt reduction. A huge number of American churches are vulnerable to any significant economic downturn.

The highly speculative and risky nature of this expansion causes us to establish foolish precedents. Many lenders now require that a life insurance policy be taken out against the senior pastor. Some churches encourage parishioners to buy life insurance policies that name the church as beneficiary. Churches offer trusts and annuities without adequate funds to cover default. Not only are these practices tenuous, but they border on the unethical.

The church really should not play the "ends justify the means" card when it comes to spending money on buildings, insurance, overhead, salaries, and infrastructure. Most churches do not need or use most of the space and property they have. Facility/plant usage surveys indicate that between 40 and 75 percent of most church space is used less than two hours per week. A large number of congregations that underutilize existing space are seeking ways to expand. It is like a form of dementia.

Americans are enamored by size. Not long ago I watched three little boys happily playing with trucks in a sandbox. They made roads and set up traffic patterns and "vroomed" and "putted" merrily along. Then a fourth boy showed up with a monster truck—one at least twice as large as any of the other boys had. This kid plowed through the sandbox, mashing the roads and shoving all the other trucks out of its way. What was the reaction of the first three kids? They were visibly impressed and jealous at the same time. As one boy was led away by his mother, the last thing I heard him say was, "I want a truck like that!"

It is not surprising that less than 1 percent of all megachurch pastors are women. It does seem to be a gender thing that little boys love their toys and they live by two simple rules: bigger is better, and the one with the most toys wins. We may age in days, but maturity is something else. A lot of church leaders want the biggest truck with the most gadgets, bells, and whistles, and it doesn't matter how much debt we incur to get it.

Perhaps the day will come when we step back from this building frenzy and reevaluate. It shouldn't escape our notice that many of our older, larger struggling churches were the stars in the crown of previous generations. The current reality, however, is that a faithful remnant are left with the burden of maintenance and upkeep of decrepit and decaying dinosaurs. Any desire to spend money on missions is trumped by the day-to-day reality of keeping the heat and light on and saving to replace the roof and the boiler. We've been there before, we're there now, and apparently, we will be going there again.

Our uncontrollable spending in the church has one other unfortunate result; it has caused church leaders to pervert the meaning and practice of Christian stewardship. Christian stewardship—the management of all that God places in our care (both individually and collectively)—means little more than giving money to the church to most American Christians. During the twentieth century, church leaders usurped the term *stewardship campaign* to refer to an annual pledge campaign to support the church budget. The concept of stewardship became a fund-raising tool (making most people duck and run whenever the word is spoken), and a foundational aspect of Christian growth and development was robbed of all its power.

A lesson we might want to remember is that good stewardship is caught as well as taught. Leaders of local churches can hardly be upset by the poor stewardship of members when they engage in such egregious practices. Mismanagement at the top rarely promotes healthy management throughout the ranks. Setting aside firstfruits and paying as you go are two aspects of Christian generosity—those who refuse to mortgage their future always have something to share.

This is an excellent time to reflect on our stewardship at the leadership level. There are no guarantees that our Christian culture will continue along the current path. In fact, all evidence indicates that the more mobile, available, and flexible we are, the better we will be able to serve a changing world. Our buildings and property are not the gravitational center of the Christian universe. That center is out in the world, and our churches exist to teach us not to resist that pull but instead to go out and be the church in the world.

GETTING THE WORD OUT

At the heart of the Christian faith is the gift and practice of evangelism. We have received a blessing and a mandate to spread the gospel of Jesus Christ to the entire world. Christians are a people of the Word.

We know *what* we're supposed to do, but we are always struggling with *how* to do it. Relational evangelism evolved into apostleship, then into crusades (both the violent kind, in the Middle Ages, and the Billy Graham kind, in the 1900s), then into the passive act of handing out "The Four Spiritual Laws" tract. As the term *evangelism* fell into disfavor, the friendlier-sounding *faith sharing* appeared. Many Christians view evangelism as the work of the pastor, and many pastors have decided to use worship as an evangelism tool in an attempt to rise to the occasion.

How to spread the gospel of Jesus Christ, how to grow congregations, how to invite people into relationship with God, and how to equip people to live as Christian disciples will continue to guide and shape our faith. Not everyone will agree with the best way to accomplish these important tasks, but virtually no one denies their importance.

Congregations come and congregations go. Theologies evolve through time. Priorities shift, and the church reinvents itself repeatedly—constructing, deconstructing, and reconstructing.

What doesn't change is our responsibility to serve God and to get the WORD out—to a hungry, thirsty, needy world.

CHAPTER 10

THE MEDIUM *IS* THE MESSAGE

Back in 1964, Marshall McLuhan coined the phrase "the medium is the message,"[1] which has been quoted and analyzed ever since. McLuhan pointed out that, simply put, what we say is always affected by how we say it— and that often what we don't say verbally speaks louder than what we do. This brilliant insight is of critical importance to the Christian church—an entity defined by the Word (and the Word made flesh).

No one can argue that the two primary media in the Christian faith—the book we call the Bible and the man we call Jesus—are as important as the messages they convey. The Bible is at once reverentially adored and is the cause of more division and conflict than almost any other writing in existence. Debate has raged throughout history over the authenticity and authority of Scripture. Is it the word of God? Does it contain words delivered by God to receptive men and women? Is it the creation of faithful men and women struggling and striving to know and understand the mind of God? Is it a human creation or a divine revelation? Is it all of these or none of these? Tempers flare as different opinions come in contact with one another. I recall once seeing a cartoon of God seated in the clouds watching earthlings fighting over the Bible, and the caption read, "Maybe a painting would have been better . . ."

And what about Jesus himself? Jesus the Christ—half human/half divine, fully human/fully divine? Inspiring teacher, Son of God, manifestation of God's Spirit? Jew, carpenter's son, born of a virgin, just like us, just like God? The *logos*, co-eternal with God, Second Person of the Trinity, Savior, Messiah, Redeemer, propitiation for our sins? Teacher, preacher, healer, prophet, rabble-rouser, criminal? Best portrayed by Jeffrey Hunter, Max Von Sydow, Ted Neeley, Willem Dafoe, Robert Powell, or James Caviezel in movies?[2] Our fixation with the historical Jesus sometimes displaces the message he proclaimed and the meaning of the resurrection. Controversy over who Jesus "really" was has nothing to do with the wisdom and power of his teachings. Oh, but don't dare suggest that the virgin birth was actually a translation error, or that the resurrection was a staged hoax, or that Jesus wed Mary Magdalene and lived happily ever after because any or all of these ideas could utterly destroy the brilliance of his proclamations.

McLuhan was right—the medium is the message—and the way we deliver the gospel of Jesus Christ speaks volumes about who we are, what we believe, and what we truly value. Which brings us to the modern day. What is the message we are sending to the modern world about Christianity? What are the values, vision, and meaning that organized religion broadcasts to the masses?

One message is that we think highly of ourselves. We build magnificent buildings with as many comforts as we can imagine. We construct gathering places—the bigger, the better—with sanctuaries and meeting rooms and classrooms and kitchens and dining rooms and activity centers and offices and sometimes bookstores and coffee shops and restaurants. We take very good care of ourselves, and a sign of our faithfulness and success is our ability to expand and build more and bigger buildings with huge parking lots and stained glass windows and landscaping and fountains and statues. And because all these things are valuable, we need security systems and alarms and locks and bars on the windows, and sometimes fences and gates and barbed wire.

Another message is that we want others to think highly of us as well. We advertise on radio and TV and paint signs and banners and run ads on the Internet and in newspapers inviting people to visit us, to join us, and to grow with us. We emphasize hospitality and friendliness, and we work hard to capture relevant information so we can follow up and, we hope, get people to come back again. We hire high-quality staff and professional performers, and we spend time and energy developing programs and services to meet the needs of a wide variety of people, though most of the things we plan and do take place inside our buildings.

This communicates a third message—we're different. We are an oasis in a crazy world. We are God's people gathering in God's house to learn God's rules for living. We use different words, sing different kinds of songs, and engage in different kinds of behavior, generally for an hour once a week. We have our own literature, our own resources, our own symbols, our own rituals and practices, all of which you can learn as you settle in.

Another message is that you can participate on your own terms. We might ask you to pray, to attend, to give, to serve, or to study, but that is pretty much left up to you. Expectations are low, and accountability is virtually nonexistent. It doesn't make much difference whether you become a member or not because members and nonmembers are treated pretty much the same. Most of what we do is geared for individuals, and you can come and get as much or as little from us as you want.

Does all this sound cynical? It should. It reflects the thoughts, feelings, and impressions of hundreds of Christian believers in the United States who have been turned off, not by what the church says, but by what it does.[3] Among the primary criticisms of Protestant churches in America are these:

- More money is spent on buildings and property than on ministry to the world.
- More time is spent inside church buildings talking about ministry than ministry is performed out in the world.
- Churches expect people to come to them instead of seeking ways to meet people where they live.
- More time is spent condemning the behaviors of non-Christians than trying to share the love of God with them.
- Success is measured in terms of attendance and money raised (and the size of the building) not by the number of people served and the number of lives changed for the better.

Some of these criticisms may be a little harsh, but there is a humbling ring of truth to each and every one. We proclaim a message of hope and peace and justice and grace for all people, but then we spend much of our time focused on ourselves. There is a word for such behavior—saying one thing and doing another—and that word is *hypocrisy*.

Often our hypocrisy is unintentional—however, hypocrisy is in the eye of the beholder. Not long ago I received a call from a pastor in North Carolina, seeking assistance with strategic planning for his congregation. I asked him, "What is the goal or objective you want to design a plan around?"

He responded by saying, "We [the leaders of the congregation] have talked about this a lot, and we have a simple, clear objective. We want to be the biggest church in North Carolina!"

I was silent for a moment then asked, "Why do you want to be the biggest church?"

"Because then we can do more. If we were bigger, we could offer more programs and hold more services and raise more money for missions," he proudly explained.

"But just getting bigger doesn't guarantee any of those things," I countered. "Being the biggest church is kind of an iffy objective. In my experience, growth is a result of excellence in a particular ministry or area, not the other way around."

"See, that's how we want to be different. When you're small, you have to decide on a course of action, then pursue it and hope you grow. But if you grow first and get big enough, then you can be successful at anything you try!"

We discussed options for a while until finally, in exasperation, the pastor said, "Look, the bottom line is that if we are the biggest church, it is proof that God is blessing our ministry and that we're on the right track. Being big is a witness to the greatness of God. All we want is to be a beacon to the world that our God is an awesome God!"

I couldn't agree more. Our God is an awesome God, but the size of our church buildings and the adequacy of our parking lots and the quality of our technology don't change that fact one bit. God is as awesome in the little white clapboard chapel in New England as in the sprawling megachurch in Texas. The fact that we've confused the medium and the message is an ongoing problem that will haunt us for some time to come.

American cultural values do not help us set priorities within the church. Church planters are quick to point out that newcomers are looking for bright, clean, open, safe spaces. Nurseries and restrooms are more important than sanctuaries to church shoppers. Congregants are coming to expect professional performance quality with state-of-the-art sound and visual equipment, and a half-caff triple shot mocha frappuccino doesn't hurt, either. More and more people are looking for the church to offer them the same aesthetic experience as a mall store or fast-food restaurant. A young woman in the airplane seat next to me explained how she and her husband finally decided on a new church home: "We found a new church with ample parking, lots of entrances, and good signage, and it doesn't block our cell signal—plus services are only about forty-five minutes. It's perfect for us!" When I asked her about the church's beliefs and teachings, she didn't really know yet but figured they would pick them up over time.

How can we cope with this mind-set? Perhaps it is not an either/or solution. The wisdom of "the medium of the message" tells us that presentation matters. However, it doesn't (or shouldn't) matter *more* than the content. Leaders in Christian congregations have a valuable role to play in helping to remind people that the church as an institution is a means to an end and not an end in itself. We don't exist to pour our resources of time, energy, talent, and money into buildings and property and possessions. We create congregational settings where the church—the whole people of God in Christ—can be empowered to move through the world offering grace, comfort, mercy, light, hope, and a message of salvation. *Where* we meet is not as important as *that* we meet, but it is still important. We will be judged by our church facilities and signs, by the quality of our offerings and our leaders. We cannot escape it, but we can use it to our advantage.

It is worth listening to our critics and those who stand outside our ranks to better understand what exactly we are communicating.

Although we may believe we are sending one message, it is apparent that many people are receiving something quite different. This is not merely a rant against hypocrisy—though the case is fairly strong—but a caution against adopting the cultural value of slick, high-quality presentation over substance and content. Our resources and technologies should better enable us to present the greatest message in the world to the masses, not inadvertently mask, mediate, or massacre it.

A wonderful concept that comes from the Greek is called *synderesis*. Synderesis is the integration and alignment of intention and action—it is the opposite of hypocrisy. It was once believed to be a function of teachers and philosophers to help people bridge the gap between their articulated values—what they said they believed—and their lived values—how they actually behaved. When lived and articulated values aligned perfectly, the individual achieved synderesis. Perhaps this is a worthy concept for leaders in churches today—to achieve a synderesis of medium and message where what we say and how we say it are so closely aligned that any possible charge of hypocrisy is completely eliminated.

Notes

1. Marshall McLuhan and Lewis H. Lapham, *Understanding Media: The Extensions of Man* (New York: McGraw-Hill, 1964).
2. *King of Kings, The Greatest Story Ever Told, Jesus Christ Superstar, The Last Temptation of Christ, Jesus of Nazareth, The Passion of the Christ.*
3. General Board of Discipleship of The United Methodist Church, "Christian Seeker Study," 2004–2007.

CHAPTER 11

VAMPIRE CHRISTIANITY

I am a Christian. I love God, and I love the church. I wish everyone could know the true satisfaction that comes from relationship to God in Christ, being wonderfully embraced in Christian community and engaged in meaningful service to others. But I also resonate with people who tell me that Christians are scary, scary people. Just last week,[1] a young woman named Tricia told me that she was hiding from the church she visited one month earlier with a friend of hers. They were met in the parking lot by a "valet from the parking ministry," who took their car, while a "faith friend" ushered them into the entryway of a huge open garden. In short order, pamphlets, a coffee mug, a refrigerator magnet, a pictorial directory, a copy of the church newsletter, and a brochure of "service opportunities" were shoved into Tricia's hands. At the end of a long line of tables, another young man, Tim, popped out to offer her a tote bag emblazoned with the church name and logo, and to introduce himself as their personal "worship guide." Tim marched Tricia to the cappuccino bar, where she was given a complimentary beverage (offered exclusively to first-time visitors) and then on to the bookstore and gift shop. In the gift shop Tricia was invited to enter a contest for an all-expenses-paid vacation to the Bahamas (no purchase necessary), compliments of the tour company that booked Holy Land visits for the church. What Tricia didn't know was that this entry captured all the necessary information—e-mail, phone number, address, and so forth—for the church to pinpoint her whereabouts better than a global positioning system. After an hour-and-a-half service that Tricia described as "loud and busy," a small cadre of women near her age descended on her and invited her to a "talk time" at the church's café and restaurant. Tricia tried a half-dozen times to decline the offer but found herself seated at a table while Brenda, the leader of the gang, peppered her with personal questions and asked her about her relationship with Jesus.

Tricia went on to tell that by the time she got home, two messages were already waiting on her answering machine, thanking her for coming to church and inviting her to attend a variety of mid-week "options." When she opened her e-mail, she found she had been added to literally dozens of listservs at the church. While sorting and deleting her e-mail, she heard a knock at the door. She opened the door to a bouquet of "welcome flowers, with a chocolate." "At first, I thought it was funny," Tricia remembered, "but then it got annoying, then surreal to the point where I wondered if I could get a restraining order against the church. They wouldn't leave me alone. I thought about having 'fresh meat' tattooed to my forehead and auctioning myself off to the highest bidder."

This humorous tale is an extreme example—most of our churches still don't do much of anything to greet, engage, or follow up with visitors. However, it does illustrate a problem in the church, and one that turns off a significant number of potential Christian disciples who could benefit from relating to our churches: feeling as if they are prey and the church is the predator. Most people do want connection—a place where they will fit in and belong, but they also want the space and time and safety in which to decide for themselves. Often, congregational leaders mistake hospitality for guerrilla warfare aimed at capturing converts. Instead, leaders might adopt a more holistic approach to hospitality, such as that suggested by Robert Kegan and Lisa Laskow Lahey: "The essence of hospitality is located not in a warm smile and a hearty handshake, but in the ability to create a meaningful shared space in which our attentions and intentions are aligned."[2]

Jamie, a medical student, shares some of Tricia's feelings about the church. "Most churches I visit start eyeing me from the moment I walk in. It's like I am a target or something—a trophy or a prize they want to win. I never feel that they care about me, only about keeping my warm body in the pew." Jamie is a devout Christian—one who prays daily, studies the Scripture regularly, tithes his income to help poor and homeless people, and donates his skills and services to area clinics. He is also what many church gurus call *unchurched.*

"I have tried. I really have. I want to be part of a church, but the ones here are so creepy. They either focus so much on getting new people that they ignore the people they have, or they are so focused on the people inside the church that they don't want to have anything to do with anyone outside the church. It's weird. Some of the churches here are *huge.* I mean, the buildings and the number of people—it's like walking into a hotel or mall. I guess I get intimidated. I just want to find a place where I can learn to be more like Jesus. I don't want to join some Christian company."

The feeling of being hunted is not uncommon among people who are seeking Christian community but who are discontented with current church offerings. Unfortunately, denominations and large independent churches do nothing to dispel the notion. Growth goals, new member campaigns, advertising programs, hospitality training, and fund-raising all place a premium on getting numbers up. Visitors and outsiders are painfully aware that they constitute the coveted growth potential, mission field, or the flattering great unwashed.

Years ago, I participated in a conversation with young adults talking about what they wished they could find in a church and what they disliked about the current options. Two young men, Josh and Matt, sought metaphors to describe how they felt. This is part of their conversation:

> JOSH: I don't know. It's like you're an outsider—like you don't really belong when you go into a church.
>
> MATT: Yeah, it's like a club, somebody else's club, like they're all part of something that you just stumble into.
>
> JOSH: Or like a coven, like vampires, you know? Like they're looking for a sacrifice and you're it.
>
> MATT: No, not vampires; vampires go after their prey. Churches aren't like vampires; they're Venus flytraps. They look harmless on the outside, and they won't bother you if you don't bother them, but step inside and *bam*. Watch out!

Many Christians may not like being compared to vampires or Venus flytraps, but both young men have the right to their opinions, and as I have shared this story over the years, many people inside the church feel that they are pretty accurate. We often do lie in wait for fresh meat, spending more time strategizing ways to get more people to come to us than ways we can take Christ into the world.

Even people inside the church report feeling preyed upon. It is too common for longtime church members to lament that they feel as if all the church wants from them is their "time, talent, and treasure." A pastor's spouse shared the following with me: "My wife and I fell behind in our giving to the church—we have three kids in college right now, and money is very tight—and believe it or not, they sent us a dunning letter. Listen to what it says:

> We want to remind you of the promise you made to God, to your church, and to yourself. Giving is a crucial part of Christian discipleship. Your church cannot be a faithful steward of its resources unless you are a faithful steward of yours. Please bring your financial commitment up-to-date as soon as possible to avoid further action on the part of your church.

"Can you believe this? I stormed to the finance chair and told him this was completely unacceptable. At first he thought I was just talking about its being sent to the pastor, but then he caught on that I thought it was inappropriate to do at all. You know what he said? He said, 'But it has been really effective, and the number of deadbeats is way down.'"

Many of our congregations use a language of commitment—inspirational-sounding words about service and mission and discipleship when what they really want is support for the status quo. This is not true of all churches, but the church in this example—according to the man telling the story—does very little beyond its own walls. The greater vision for ministry is to have more people sit in the pews on Saturday night and Sunday morning, not to mobilize more people to live their faith in daily life.

A layperson from another church complained, "My church just takes and takes and takes. Anybody who makes the mistake of volunteering for something just once is expected to do more and more.

Nothing is ever good enough. I finally had to leave the church, I was feeling so drained and dry."

These stories are not at all unusual, and they reflect a mind-set that is less than healthy in the long term. People are not merely resources to use up and discard. Members of a congregation do not exist solely to support the church. It is a reciprocal relationship. People give to and through the church, and the church equips and supports them to live more faithfully in the world. Many people who serve in the inner circles of church leadership report a feeling that they are expected to give and work so that less committed members don't have to. Over time, this breeds resentment and burnout. A retired teacher told me, "I worked for my church for years—gave the very best I had to minister to others. When I retired, I went through a really tough time emotionally, and I needed my church to minister to me instead of expecting me to do more. When I expressed this to others, I was told I was being selfish and spiritually immature. It broke my heart."

Vampire Christianity occurs whenever the institution takes and takes and takes and gives little or nothing in return. The need of the institution to receive should never be more important than the needs of individuals to be nurtured, strengthened, equipped, and empowered to live as faithful Christian disciples. Evidence of vampire Christianity exists whenever the focus is on the behaviors of participants instead of the grounding foundational values beneath the behaviors. For example, when a congregation focuses on giving instead of generosity, it is usually trying to get people to give to the church instead of helping them grow in faith. When our focus is on training greeters instead of extending radical hospitality, we are not so interested in transforming people's engagement with each other as we are in getting new members or attendees. When we use worship services as a tool for evangelism instead of helping the believing body of Christ honor and praise God, then we are crossing the line toward blood-suckerism. Every time we make the church about the institution over and above community in Christ, we are practicing a form of vampire Christianity.

Churches that are vital, healthy, and truly transformative spend very little time trying to recruit members, entice participants, raise money, or craft a catchy slogan. Congregations where people are deeply engaged in the journey of faith, growing as disciples, discovering their gifts, and being equipped for meaningful service are well supported, provided for, and led. They focus more on what they have to share with others instead of constantly working to get people to give things to them. It is a very simple distinction—if the church is more concerned about others than itself, it is healthy and alive, but if it is more concerned with its own needs over the needs of others, all it lacks are fangs and a cape.

Notes

1. A sentence beginning "Just last week . . . " in a book like this has absolutely no meaning, but it indicates that this is a frequent and not unusual occurrence.
2. Robert Kegan and Lisa Laskow Lahey, *How the Way We Talk Can Change the Way We Work* (San Francisco: Jossey-Bass, 2001), p. 190.

CHAPTER 12

FAITH SHOVING

THE NEW EVANGELISM

"Do you know Jesus Christ as your personal Lord and Savior?" the smallish woman asked as I pushed on toward my connecting flight.

I looked at the woman, startled, and attempted to ignore her.

She persisted. "You may think I'm weird, but I need you to know that you're in danger of eternal damnation if you don't accept Jesus. *Today!*"

I stopped, fixed my gaze on hers, and said, "Thanks, ma'am, but I am a United Methodist pastor." Assuming that would settle the issue, I started to move away.

Following in my wake, the woman cried, "Yes, but are you saved?"

Stopping short, I emphasized, "I just told you. I'm a minister!"

Wide-eyed, the woman said, "But you said you were Methodist. I want to know if you're Christian."

Many people in our country wonder whether Methodists—or any members of the mainline denominations—are truly Christian. This notion comes from confusion over what really constitutes Christian belief. There are so many flavors of Christianity that it gets confusing. When I was growing up, Protestants and Catholics looked at each other with deep suspicion, each holding that the other was somehow defective in their faith. With the rise of evangelicalism and the Pentecostal undercurrent, being saved, born again, convicted in the Spirit, and knowing Jesus Christ as *personal* Lord and Savior became further differentiations of merit. I grew up with a number of friends who believed that the mark of true Christianity was the ability to speak in tongues—though there was some disagreement about what tongues actually were. I had a friend in college who was slain in the Spirit and afterward could not associate with me due to my defiled and unrepentant state.

When I moved to Tennessee, I witnessed what some label guerrilla evangelism—chasing people down, cornering them, and then forcing tracts and witnessing upon them while they look around, hoping for rescue. I attended a conference for children and youth where they were told that they could not please God and go to heaven unless they were telling others about their faith. The leaders of the event gave each young person five hundred "Four Spiritual Laws" tracts and told the attendees that they could not come back to youth group until they had given away every one. A young adult conference also emphasized the importance of witnessing, and one prominent leader stated, "Don't take no for an answer. If you have to hire people to physically hold people down, do it. The word of God must not be denied. First, you offer it. Then, you impose it. And if people still do not care to listen, you take it upon yourself to cram it down their throats. In a godless age, it is the least you can do."

I am of two minds here. It is great to believe so deeply in something that you want everyone—especially loved ones—to share it. On the other hand, it helps explain why so many non-Christians feel that Christians are arrogant, pushy, tedious, and scary. Evangelism is important, but what we mean by evangelism—and its warm, fuzzy twenty-first-century equivalent, faith sharing—requires careful reexamination.

There are many wonderful metaphors for the Christian faith, but weapon is not one of them. There is little or no defense for using the Bible to batter people over the head and shoulders, bludgeoning them into belief and submission—though it has been used this way for centuries. The grace of God is a gift, and it should be offered as such. People have a right to accept it or reject it. When people accept it, we should feel joyful and glad and celebrate with them. When people reject it, we have the right to feel sad, but we do not have the right to attack and revile them. It is our responsibility to proclaim the good news, to scatter the seed that is the word of God, but it is not our job to force people to accept it.

When I attended a program at a well-known independent church, two young women approached me and other people in my group. They offered pocket-sized New Testaments, and I held up my hands and declined taking one.

One of the young women shrieked, "Take one, take one!" and threw one at me, hitting me in the cheek.

I walked over to her and said, "What are you doing?"

She looked rather abashed and said, "I didn't mean to hit you, but I wanted you to have a Bible."

I said, "I have a lot of Bibles at home and didn't need to take another one. I have that right. I don't have to take something if I don't want to."

With a pout, she said, "I didn't know you already had one. I'm supposed to make sure people have a Bible, whether they want one or not."

Something has gotten lost in translation. It is one thing to be so excited, so on fire, so pumped up that you cannot help telling people what is great in your life, but it is something quite different to shoulder an obligation to force a set of beliefs, creeds, or scriptures on people you know nothing about. Evangelism is not an onerous task to perform. Evangelism, at its very best, is an opportunity to build and strengthen relationships where the transformative good news of Jesus Christ is natural, normal, and reasonable to share.

This truth is simple—so simple, in fact, that it is often overlooked. People relate stories of those who had a significant impact on their lives, people who modeled a way of living and believing, people who gave something special to them that made all the difference in the world. Evangelism was not effective because of words spoken, tracts handed out, or a persuasive script followed but because of a meaningful relationship. People earn the right to be heard by first caring about and respecting the people they want to speak to.

Churches grow not primarily because of a preacher or a program or a membership crusade, but because real, ordinary men and women invite friends, family, and colleagues to come to their church. They want people to come to church because they love God, they love the people, and they think their church is something special. The most effective invitations are made from the foundation of meaningful relationships.

Literally hundreds of books have been written on evangelism—most of them aimed at training Christian believers to talk to the "unchurched." Some are about faith sharing—ways of working God and Jesus and church into everyday, ordinary conversations. There are programs for whole congregations on inviting people to church, learning hospitality, training greeters and ushers, and cold-calling new residents in the community. The success rates of these books and resources vary—from poor to not so good. The reason? Faith sharing and authentic evangelism are not a church program. They are not things we learn to do; they are extensions of who we are. When we are transformed by the love of God, we cannot help sharing it with everyone we meet. And we do not always share it in words. We share it in our thoughts, behaviors, and actions.

Perhaps the most egregious error on the part of many well-meaning Christians is that evangelism is not primarily about creating new church members. The invitation to enter into a lifelong relationship with the living God in Jesus Christ is the heart and soul of evangelism. Getting people to join our church is not. Too many evangelists are nothing more than thinly disguised church recruiters.

That is why many people outside established churches feel that they are prey and American Christians are hunters. A growing number of non-Christians are more and more defensive as they feel literally attacked by church members. These disenchanted outsiders do not feel that Christians are concerned with their well-being; they feel that Christians have an aggressive agenda that they want to force on the world.

It is an interesting time of contradictory feast and famine. A cultural perception is that conservative evangelical Christians are becoming more pushy and pervasive—influencing politics, economics, globalization, the media, and education—while a majority of church leaders lament that the message is not being spread and that people are not willing to take their faith out onto the front lines of the culture wars. Can both perspectives be true?

Seemingly, yes. A pseudo-Christian political agenda has surfaced in America that uses faith in Jesus as a tool and platform for manipulation and populist pretense (what is good according to Christians will be good for everyone). It is a very "in" thing to be Christian and to use the faith to further personal goals and objectives. Many groups and organizations that promote good Christian values are only nominally Christian, using whatever means possible to gain social influence. These voices employ a stunning pick-and-choosism crusading for the unconditional sanctity of life (anti-abortion, anti-choice, anti-gay) except in arbitrary cases (stem cell research to end terminal and debilitating diseases, capital punishment, gun control). This presentation of the Christian faith is not about the saving, redeeming, sanctifying, and unifying love of God. This is not evangelism—it is a rude form of evangelicalism, designed to command and control from a narrow minority perspective.

The problem is that this minority is defining the majority. The vocal and aggressive few command a great deal of airtime on television and radio. Peripheral lay voices like Rush Limbaugh and Ann Coulter tell the mainstream what it means to be a Christian, to be a moral person, to live by "family values." Sadly, people listen to such voices and accept them at face value. They rarely question why political pundits and media personalities are taking it upon themselves to teach things they actually know very little about. These folks spout personal opinions as if they were gospel truths, and way too many listeners perpetuate the fallacy.

The solution to this situation rests inside established Christian churches. It is up to congregational leaders to redeem the concept of evangelism and rescue faith sharing from the bastardization of the political religious right. To do this, we need to stop using evangelism as a tool for growing our congregations. We cannot criticize the secular culture for usurping and corrupting the Christian faith when we are guilty of doing it. We need to teach, encourage, and equip people to share their faith stories. We need to make sure that people understand that the invitation to having a relationship with Christ is about the person we invite, not about us. We need to help people value the blessings they receive enough to want to share those gifts with others. We need to remember that the gospel is good news and not some doctrinaire agenda to cram down people's throats.

I met a man who sheepishly asked me whether I was a Christian. I replied that I was, and he nodded and quietly said, "That's good. That's real good." He sat in silence for a moment, then told me, "I wasn't a Christian, but I met a lady who brought me sandwiches in the afternoons when I was out of work and out on the street. She did it every time she saw me. After a few weeks, I asked her why she did it. She said it was because she was a Christian and she believed that feeding hungry people was what God wanted her to do."

The man shuffled his feet, then went on, "I'm working now, and I don't take her sandwiches anymore, but I did take Christ into my life. I want to be like that woman who fed me, and I want everybody to know that it's because of Jesus."

This is evangelism. This is faith sharing. Taking Jesus Christ with us wherever we go so that lives are saved and transformed, and the love of God spreads like a glorious virus. You don't have to force goodness, and you don't have to shove God in people's faces. When you live it, it is impossible to ignore.

CHAPTER 13

ÜBERFAITH VERSUS INTERFAITH

Three short stories. Three somewhat embarrassing, though common stories. Stories about how well-meaning sincere Christians relate to members of other faiths. Stories about ways we slam the door on the grace of God and earn for ourselves a reputation as narrow-minded and ignorant.

Story #1—Pretending You like Them

A young, very successful emerging pastor shared stories from his ministry where he ventured into the "real world" to talk to people about Jesus Christ. He recounted tales of meeting nonbelievers, occult believers, and believers of world religions. He told two stories—one about meeting a young couple of pagans who dabbled in the Wiccan faith and another about two young Buddhist men he met in a coffee shop. He emphasized to the group—mostly pastors and ministers to young adults—the importance of meeting and talking to these people: "These are the people that Jesus died for, and they are the people who need saving." He told us the key to saving them was twofold: first, we need to learn to pretend to like these people, and second, we need to invite them into open, honest dialogue so that we can convince them that they are wrong. I looked around the room and noticed that people were furiously taking notes and nodding their heads.

I hope I don't have to point out what bothered me about this young church growth guru's instructions. First, I do not believe that God calls us, expects us, or wants us to pretend to like anyone. Deceiving people is not a cornerstone of authentic Christian evangelism. People who have a heart for God and seek to live as Christian disciples don't have to fake it. Second, people who have the agenda of convincing others that they are wrong are not really interested in open, honest dialogue. Hammering home a message that you are right and that others are wrong is a flawed definition of dialogue. It is one thing to share different ideas about life, meaning, eternity, and existence but something very different to strategize ways to win a debate.

Story #2—Being Right Is the Most Important Thing

At a conference discussing the Great Commission—"Go therefore and make disciples of all nations, baptizing them in the name of the Father and of the Son and of the Holy Spirit" (Matt 28:19)—conversation turned to the challenges of disciple making in the modern world. One venerable older United Methodist voice spoke up to say that the problem wasn't an unreceptive world but Christians who lack the courage and conviction to share their faith. I, innocently and ignorantly, piped in that one of the factors making the Great Commission difficult was the changing face of religion in America—that as more faiths encountered one another, it required delicacy to present one's faith without disrespecting the faith of others. The grand older Methodist looked at me over the top of his glasses, pursed his lips, and said, "I fail to see why that is any kind of problem."

"Well, Christians definitely have things of value to share with members of other faiths, but we need to be mindful of the things we can learn from others as well," I explained.

"You have named the crux of the matter. We do have something of value to tell the world, but you are in error when you say they have things of value to teach us. When you are right, you are right, and we are right. We have the way, the truth, and the life, and we have nothing to learn from people who follow false gods and idols."

As no one came to my aid or offered a counteropinion, I let it drop (at the time . . . obviously, it still bugs me or I wouldn't be writing about it now) and held my tongue from that time forward. Having been blessed with the good news of Jesus Christ, I love opportunities to share my beliefs and to discuss them with others—with those who agree as well as with those who do not. At no time, however, do I believe that my beliefs, my opinions, and my interpretations are so perfect that I have all the answers. I believe that humility demands not only a gracious presentation of my beliefs but also a willingness to listen to others. For me, the logic of refusing to listen to the people we wish to save breaks down quickly. If we refuse to meet people where they are, understand their thinking and beliefs, and offer them the most basic respect, how will we ever earn the respect or credibility that would make them listen to us at all? The ability to share the good news of Jesus Christ often requires that we forge a relationship with people quite different from ourselves.

Story #3—Destroying the Enemy in Christian Love

Soon after the tragedy of 9/11, I attended a national youth conference where one speaker made the point that terrorists have gained power in our world because Christians have failed in their responsibility to spread the gospel. She emphasized that when the world resembles the realm of God, there is no place for terrorism—that if people experienced God's love, violence would not be needed to solve our problems. Following the presentation, the teenagers regrouped in discussion cells to talk about what they heard. Two adults facilitated each cell. I sat in on one group just to see how the speaker's message was heard.

The conversation took an odd turn quickly. One young girl said how scared she was that other people in the world hated Christians and wanted to kill us. Another member of the group responded by saying that Christians had gotten too soft, allowing nonbelievers to gain political and military might. A third young woman said that she didn't understand why people of other religions didn't want to go to heaven and why they chose to go to hell instead. I waited for one of the adults to jump in, but both remained silent.

One young man stated, "Talking isn't ever going to be good enough. We need to deal with them the way they are dealing with us. If we would wipe out all the wrong religions, then the earth would become exactly like heaven." At last, an adult chimed in, offering the following wisdom: "And this is why it is so important to support our president and our military. When the rest of the world sees how God blesses America, people will realize that you can't get away with attacking Christians."

I realize that this faith worldview is foreign to my own. It feels very Old Testament rather than specifically Christian. I have never been a subscriber to the "might makes right" school of religion, but beyond that, I have difficulties with the more basic idea that violence is ever the appropriate course of action to *prove* the love of God. Beating the hell out of people seems somehow inferior to loving the hell out of them. Even if we truly believe others are evil, destroying them completely eliminates any chance of conversion and redemption. Killing enemies is really hard to defend with a New Testament theology.

The modern reality is a global community, filled with varied worldviews, values, and religions. The adherents of every religion believe that their faith is the one, true, "right" faith. Being right, and by extension, believing others are wrong, does not automatically mean that you must respond to others with violence. It does not mean that you have the right to disrespect, disregard, or attack them. It does not grant the privilege of treating others with contempt, derision, or annihilation. Perhaps primitive, brutish people believe that bullying and assault are appropriate, but fortunately, Christians cannot fall into these categories. Attacking enemies and assaulting outsiders are simply not allowed (yes, I know I'm being facetious).

The challenges of conflicting faiths and incompatible religions will grow, not recede, in the decades to come. Christian believers are faced with at least four choices—described brilliantly by H. Richard Niebuhr in 1951—to help us cope with a truly interfaith world.[1]

The first choice is to view Christianity as the Überfaith—Christ, and by extension, Christian belief, is *above culture*, superior in every way to worldly beliefs, customs, and practices. This perspective creates a vertical duality—things of God are holy and good, while things of earth are secular and less worthy. For many Christian believers, this point of view sets our church in a position of superiority. Adopting this view closes the door on any real collaboration and conversation. There is nothing to be gained by dialogue, and working alongside proponents of other belief systems might give people the wrong idea. Better to isolate ourselves and claim the exclusive dominance of our way of thinking. What Niebuhr described and how it has been interpreted and applied may be quite different, but the fundamental dualism—the critical "us versus them"—remains consistent.

The second choice is to view all other religious belief systems as threats to the truth—non-Christians are not a mission field, but our enemies. This constitutes a horizontal dualism—Christ and Christian believers *against culture*. Those who subscribe to other religions—or no religion (go figure)—are out to get us, and the best approach is to defeat any and all opponents. If this cannot be done through superior intellect and argument, then we may take up arms to physically defeat those who will not receive correction. The motivation of this mind-set is conquest, to find some way for Christ to win the world and eliminate the competition.

An equally troubling third option is the co-opting of Christ and Christian teachings by the dominant culture. When we find Christ *in culture*, we end up being taught our beliefs by the likes of Joan Osborne, Roma Downey, Mel Gibson, and the History Channel. Jesus becomes a pop sensation, and the gospel is sanitized, secularized, and sound-bited into insipid paraphrased versions and abridged audiobooks. Sentimental and saccharine TV spots aim to make people understand that the church of Jesus Christ is a happy, friendly, comfy place, just like grandma's house.

A fourth option, however, is to live in the power and confidence of the Christian faith, understanding that there are value and truth to our beliefs that cannot be undermined by disagreement. Our witness in the world is to model a way of living, thinking, loving, and believing that affirms the basic goodness of all God's people—even those who don't see things our way. Living as a Christian witness *within a diverse and pluralistic global culture* is our highest goal; we rejoice when people join us in our beliefs, and we respectfully acquiesce to those who choose not to.

In Jesus' day, many chose not to believe and follow him. He taught that there would always be those who would choose another way. The parable of the Sower of Seed reminds us that our primary job is to plant the seeds, to spread good news, and to make the gospel available to everyone we meet. There is nothing about tilling the soil, feeding and watering, weeding, and eventually reaping. That is all up to God. Faithful Christian disciples sow the seed, in whatever ways possible, in thought, word, and deed.

Christians are not better than everyone else, just luckier. When we realize we are fortunate, not superior, we share our faith in a very different way. When we acknowledge that God is greater than any one belief system, we realize that God may be reaching many different people in many different ways.[2] Even a cursory reading of Hindu, Buddhist, Islamic, and many other religions shows that some universal truths and beliefs transcend culture, race, or creed. Learning all we can of the great thinking of the ages throughout the world is not a danger to Christian orthodoxy, but an acknowledgment that our God is an awesome God, and that great ideas belong to everyone.

Notes

1. H. Richard Niebuhr, *Christ and Culture* (New York: Harper, 1951).
2. This should not be such a difficult concept for a people who ride the coattails of another faith. Judaism and Christianity share much in common, but there are also dramatically different beliefs, customs, and practices. It is of no great trauma for Christians to believe that God communicated to Jewish people in very different ways in the time of the Law and the Prophets than God communicated to Jesus and Paul at the dawn of the Christian faith.

Missing the Point

It is difficult being critical without being negative. Church growth, prepackaged church programs, stewardship campaigns, cutting edge technology, and mass marketing techniques aren't bad in and of themselves, but in all too many instances they are displacing more important concerns.

All of these things—as well as the myriad bells and whistles of contemporary Christian "churchiosity"—are merely tools for the real work of the body of Christ. Something has gone seriously wrong when the vision of a local congregation is "paying off the $250,000 debt on our art and statues" or "stealing the media consultant from XYZ church" (both of these are visions I have encountered recently) instead of faithful ministry to others.

Similarly, when Christian leaders become celebrities and cult figures, something has gone seriously wrong. As communities of faith, we cease seeking our meaning, purpose, and direction from God and the guidance of the Spirit, and we look for salvation at leadership institutes, on DVDs, television, or the *New York Times* bestseller list.

Our answers aren't "out there" somewhere but within the hearts, minds, gifts, and spirit of the assembled congregation—working together prayerfully and faithfully.

When the church is about anything other than God and serving God's people and creation, then, somehow, we've missed the point.

CHAPTER 14

EMERGENT DETERGENT

New movements are messy—even new variations on old movements. In the Christian church, new movements launch constantly as correctives to perceived shortcomings, wrong turns, and heresies within the mainstream. The old adage "There's nothing new under the sun" (thanks, Ecclesiastes!) is never more true than when applied to religious movements.

Which is why the current emerging/emergent church movement (or whatever its proponents want to call it—for simplicity's sake I will adopt the popular *emerging*) is so perplexing. I have attended only a few conferences, but I have read several books, and I scratch my head at the concept that this is something new or different—which is not to say that it is unimportant. So many of the leading voices appear to lack a historical sense, though they frame many of their concepts in terms of a return to an earlier, ill-defined Christianity—often labeled Acts 2 or first century—as if some pristine model existed in a mythological bygone day. We need to keep in mind that we rarely create a viable future by pursuing a nonexistent past.

A central tenet of the emerging church movement is its openness and flexibility—which is viewed as both its major strength and its fundamental weakness. There is a real "anything goes" feel to emerging gatherings—a sense that God is revealing to us a new, fresh, and relevant future. At the same time, the lack of knowledge of Christian history, theology, and earlier emergings makes the whole movement seem ignorant and uninformed. There is nothing discussed at these conferences that Luther, the Wesleys, George Fox, Walter Rauschenbusch, Karl Barth, and literally hundreds of other Christian thinkers haven't raised before—often in more depth and clarity. What the emerging church movement is saying is really good, but it has all been said before.

A second shortcoming of the movement is that many of its leaders are very happy to be in the spotlight. The main messages of the emerging church are simple—we live in a different world, where people are looking for different things; old structures and organizations have lost focus; the church is not a building; the reason the church exists is to serve others, not itself; we live in an experience-based (heart) culture rather than our parents' reason-based (head) culture—and it doesn't take much time to say them. Prominent voices in the emerging church movement sing the same songs again and again, rehashing and recycling the same tired messages in book after book. The literature from the late twentieth century was fresh and interesting; but the publications—both print and Web—of the past few years are derivative and stale. The dearth of new information has led some emerging writers to stretch their message into strange—and poorly researched—directions, claiming that we are just now coming to understand what Jesus *really* meant because we are finally enlightened enough to do so! Yikes.

One last lament I share about the emerging church is that it has ceased to emerge and has been usurped by the mainline.

When the emerging voices were calling from the fringes, there was an air of danger and intrigue—the veil had been lifted, the curtain was ripped away, and we were revealed with all our flaws and failings exposed. Emerging voices decried the compromises that the megachurch was making. Emerging voices accused the mainline of becoming inbred and incestuous (figuratively speaking). Emerging voices called for a simplification of the gospel message—a clarion call to love God and neighbor and to make the world a better place. Emerging voices screamed for us to get our noses out of dusty books (in newly printed books) and get out into the real world to put our faith into action. The summons to walk the talk was coming from the edge, not the center, and it was exciting.

Now, emerging churches are becoming megachurches, and megachurches are calling themselves emerging/emergent. Now, mainline Protestant pastors are adopting the messages of the emerging church and are modifying, manipulating, and marginalizing them to fit the institutional church. Now, almost any church that serves anyone outside its four walls is claiming to be emerging. It's kind of like watching your parents dress, act, and speak like teenagers. The ick factor is *way* high.

Criticizing the emerging church phenomenon is too easy, however. Critics slam emerging leaders for lack of clarity, sloppy use of jargon, misappropriation of the postmodern label (refer to chapter 3), theological license, lack of coherence and structure, and a plethora of other foibles. Fine. Almost every one of these criticisms has merit, but they also miss the point. The reason the emerging church is emerging is that there is significant dissatisfaction with the status quo. The divide between what church *is* and what church *could be* is too great for many modern Christians. Voices from a broad spectrum of theological and spiritual perspectives are asking serious questions about the mission and purpose of Christianity in the twenty-first century. A rising tide of concern that the church is irrelevant and inwardly focused is leading men and women from both inside and outside the formal church structures to seek a more faithful alternative. It really doesn't matter that we've been here before—obviously, things didn't work out so well before or we wouldn't be here again.

The emerging church movement is stuck on the event horizon of a theological black hole (cool image, huh?). It has gotten too overblown—it is a simple, serious message, but a message that taken too seriously will bog down and disappear (black hole). If it keeps hypermarketing itself, it takes on a circus feel and loses credibility (drifting in space, to complete the metaphor). If it stays on the fringe, it lacks a widespread audience; if it slides into the mainstream, it becomes irrelevant.

True emerging visionaries love the paradox and tension. They don't mind that the McLarens and Bells hop into the spotlight—that merely allows the fringe thinkers to stay fringe. The more popular a few stars become, the easier it is to fly beneath the radar. The last thing real emerging minds want to see is the institutionalization of the emerging church—which is why they avoid the huge conferences like the plague.

One popular fear about the emerging church movement is that it is essentially about undermining established churches and allowing theologically uninformed malcontents to reshape church in a form they prefer. There is almost no evidence to support such a fear. An honest appraisal of emerging topics reveals that they are insightful and honest; rarely are criticisms lodged without commensurate suggestions for alternatives and solutions. The vast majority of emerging church supporters want to open dialogue, allow for much greater diversity in theological reflection and scriptural interpretation, and shift emphasis off all the things we shouldn't be doing onto all the things we should be doing. It is somewhat amazing that the movement has come under such severe attack. Perhaps the fact that so many of the most vocal proponents of the emerging movement have also been the least knowledgeable and articulate has created unnecessary misunderstandings.

The emerging church movement is not going away—however, it will evolve, and within a generation it will have a different name and different leaders will be associated with it. Always and ever, men and women emerge from the fringes to challenge the status quo. Moses was one of the earliest emerging church leaders, listening to a burning bush that seemed to interest no one else. Jesus was one of the loudest, strongest emerging church voices ever heard, and the entire world changed because of it. Martin Luther, John Wesley, William Seymour, Jonathan Edwards, and many others shared the "burning bush" mentality from inside the institution to turn aside and seek a better way. Dozens of men and women outside the mainstream called for change in the nineteenth century that led to the Social Gospel movement, and similar fringe voices called for the church to hit the streets for homeless people and hippies during the Jesus movement of the 1960s. As long as people look to the church to live up to the will of God, there will be an emerging church—a church suffering the birth pangs of change, transformation, and growth from something less to something more.

In each generation, outsiders call the church to account. Disaffected insiders challenge the status quo. These watchdogs serve as cleansing showers (floods), passing through and washing away the sediment that coats and covers and obscures. They encourage us to scrub away the dirt and get back down to the real shine. They inspire us to clean up our act. It very well may be that these emerging voices in each era are the supply of living water that God sends to make sure the church stays healthy and fresh.

CHAPTER 15

SOMETHING OLD, SOMETHING NEW, SOMETHING BORROWED, SOMETHING BLUE

We have developed an interesting definition of leadership in the Christian church. It goes something like this: "Effective church leaders adopt popular practices, programs, processes, and procedures of more successful leaders." It doesn't take a genius to realize that this defines not leadership, but "followership." Doing what someone else has already done doesn't put us at the cutting edge. The dilemma of modern congregational leadership is that all the good stuff has already been done.

It is indeed difficult to be an innovator in a 2,000-year-old organization. Most claims to newness in the church are questionable at best. Certainly, the application of new technologies may make things look different, but appearances are often deceiving. American culture doesn't make it any easier, either. Ours is a world enamored with the novel, the new, and the never-seen-before. This results in a constant quest for the next big thing. In my lifetime, there have been numerous fads and next big things in the church. Late in the 1950s there was a rush to add gymnasiums to church facilities. Multipurpose rooms combining sanctuary, classrooms, and fellowship halls were big in the 1960s, 1970s, and 1980s. "Contemporary worship"[1] got hotter than Pet Rocks and Rubik's Cubes. Today, there is a rush to build Christian life centers, place information kiosks in our narthexes and entryways, and dispense Christian cappuccino. Projection screens, sound boards, church parlors, libraries, bookstores—these and many other "innovations"—emerge like clockwork. Once they are successful in one or two locations, everyone wants to get on board. Less leadership than lemming-instinct, this kind of congregational faddism is as old as the faith.

Many congregational leaders are looking for a magic bullet that will solve the problems of declining numbers, lack of funds, empty classrooms, and poor attendance. The thinking goes, "If we can just find the right program or offer the right kind of service or hold the right kind of campaign, then success will be ours." And so we go a-huntin'. We don't have far to look.

Effective church leaders love to brag. There is a pervasive "we did it, you can too" mentality throughout the church. We love to tell our stories, pointing out how we moved from mediocrity to success. There are literally thousands of books, resources, videos, and programs designed to help churches do what they do more effectively. Most are prescriptive—*12 Keys to Effective Ministry, Seven Steps to a Better Church, 101 Ways to Fund Your Budget, 40 Days of Purpose.* Some are informational—like most Sunday school and Bible study materials. A few are practical—like Mother's Day Out and Stephen's Ministries programs.

The prescriptive programs share many similarities with diet books. Many people look for a diet book that will produce almost magical results—great weight loss with the least amount of sacrifice, discomfort, and bother. The reason there are so many diets is that they offer so many chances to find the right one. The often overlooked aspect of the diet industry is that its ongoing popularity depends on its fundamental lack of success. If a diet book actually worked, then there would be no market for further diets.[2] The same is true of the church leadership publishing market. The reason that people keep buying more and more books on effective church leadership is that the last one failed to deliver worthwhile results. Over time, pastors and lay leaders become resource junkies, seeking the next fix that doesn't really fix anything.

Books are one major outlet for information, but growing in popularity are leadership institutes hosted at successful megachurches where leadership teams from across the country travel to learn at the feet of the masters. Workshops, seminars, plenary sessions, and panel discussions reveal a multitude of secrets to effective ministry. Feedback from these sessions indicates that they are popular, interesting, well designed and delivered, but four out of five participants report that they learn virtually nothing they can take home and apply.

Books and training institutes often ignore the importance of context. Each congregational setting is unique. Many programs work so well in a particular location because they match the needs, tastes, and experience of the people involved. Every church has its own history, traditions, rituals, hopes, and expectations. The resource or program that is so helpful to one church may offer nothing of value to another.

This is not news because we inherently understand that one size does *not* fit all. Congregations are complex organizations, and complex organizations defy easy answers. The effort required to create a healthy environment for spiritual formation and vital discipleship is immense. It cannot be done quickly, and any shortcuts will merely compromise the strength and durability of the community of faith.

Not everyone is seeking an innovative new direction for his or her church. An interesting countermovement is a glorification of the ancient Christian church. The central idea of this approach is that much of what modern churches do is nonessential, wasting valuable time, effort, and energy. Often leaders of this movement cite Acts 2:42-47 as their model, and they call for a return to a simpler, purer, holier time. There is merit to the desire to simplify the church, but the concept is more than just simple; it's simplistic. The experiences of a primitive, premodern group who expected the imminent return of Jesus Christ in an impoverished and oppressed culture hardly translate well to the affluent modern West where few believe Jesus is standing on the threshold. It is also worth noting that most of the early simple churches—including most that Paul established—failed within their first few decades. They were difficult to sustain then; even more so today.

Rarely does the path into the future lie in the past. It is very difficult to move forward by moving backward. Lessons can be learned from our antecedents, but it is up to us to work out our own salvation with fear and trembling. Innovation is hard, borrowing solutions from others isn't effective, and the past lacks what we need to build a future. What's left? Many churches seek answers in the shocking, the sensational, and the soup of the day.

If the messages of God's love and the gospel of Jesus Christ won't draw in crowds, then all we need to do is to find something juicy and provocative enough that will. At least once every generation, the Christian church develops a renewed interest in sex. I'm not talking about abuse or misconduct. I'm talking about the rediscovery that sex is a gift from God and that godly men and women can engage in it guilt free and for pleasure (in the comfort of the marriage bed only). Pastors get all kinds of media attention for being risqué, using "adult" language, and being open, frank, and honest. In every new iteration, pastors who broach the subject are praised for their refreshing perspectives, their courage, and their valuable contribution. These pastors hold seminars, write books, post websites, and draw in the crowds. This popularity lasts a short time, causing hot-topic pastors to seek something even more controversial (homosexuality?), fashionable (AIDS/malaria?), or urgent (terrorism/natural disaster?).

What all these approaches have in common is this: they seek external solutions to internal issues. Truly vibrant and healthy congregations have found their own answers. While the answers are unique and contextually appropriate, leaders in most of these settings share three similar stories.

First, know thyself. Congregations that have a compelling vision and purpose, clarity around gifts, skills, and opportunities, and a strong sense of identity are healthy, growing churches. The ability to say, "This is who we are, this is why we're here, and this is what we can do," is essential to congregational vitality.

Second, focus. The healthiest churches do a few things very well instead of trying to do a little of everything. Emerging from the clarity of gifts, passions, possibilities, and purpose are the priorities that guide the mission and ministry of the congregation. *How* the congregation lives in Christian community builds upon *who* it is and *what* it's for—form follows function.

Third, take the next step. Dynamic congregations are aware of their strengths and weaknesses, they know what they can do and what they cannot, and they continuously assess where they can best improve. As a congregation and as individuals, the entire church seeks ways to learn, to grow, to develop, and to mature. There is a high commitment to lifelong learning and spiritual formation internally, and a structure and plan to help people serve externally. Leaders and congregational members keep their eyes on where God might lead them next.

Each of these three orientations is flexible and adaptable to almost any context. They honor the unique character and personality of the community of faith, and they provide an important foundation upon which to build a future.

There are as many excellent solutions as there are problems. Christian Schwarz, in his seminal work on Natural Church Development, teaches that we should study not models, but principles.[3] Models indicate that there is one right way to do things, and that success depends on our ability to follow a recipe or set of instructions. Principles are more useful because they must be customized in order to be applied. The bottom line is that no one else has your answer. You have your own answer, and by God's grace and guidance, you'll find it.

Notes

1. The root meaning of *contemporary* is "with the times" or, more appropriately, "with the living." The hope is that by this definition, all of our worship is contemporary.
2. The best diet book I ever saw was called *The Last Diet Book You'll Ever Need*. It was almost four hundred pages long, but on each left-hand page, printed in block letters, were the words *Eat Less*. On the facing right-hand page were the words *Exercise More*. That's all—just the repeated instructions to eat less and exercise more. Brilliant.
3. *Natural Church Development: A Guide to Eight Essential Qualities of Healthy Churches* (Carol Stream, Ill.: Church Smart Resources, 2006).

GETTING OVER OURSELVES

One of the most offensive ideas to many Christians is that maybe the entire universe doesn't revolve around us. It just might be that in the grand scheme of things, each individual human life is relatively insignificant. This doesn't mean that God doesn't love us, and that we are not important in a small way, but it might indicate that the world won't come to an end if we were to miraculously and magically disappear. There are billions of human beings on earth today, no one less valuable or important than any others, no one more valuable, either.

If we're all truly equal in the sight of God, we ought to rethink our annoying penchant to fight over almost every disagreement, to keep accumulating and expanding, to make Christianity simplistic and palatable to the masses, and to assume that the way we do church in America is the right way for everyone else. In the nineties—both the 1890s and the 1990s—Charles Sheldon's provocative question, "What would Jesus do?" took the American Christian population by storm. The main difference between the two centuries' expressions of the WWJD phenomenon was the mass marketing that accompanied the latter. Bracelets, bumper stickers,

T-shirts, pens, coffee mugs, mouse pads, and screen savers made WWJD ubiquitous. Perhaps it's time for a new question:

WWJRDIHWTCBT?

(What Would Jesus *Really* Do If He Were to Come Back Today?)

Church as depicted in our Christian Gospels bears little resemblance to what we think of as church today. First of all, church was constantly on the move—Jesus and the boys kept traveling from place to place, taking the good news with them wherever they went. Second, church happened every day of the week, at whatever time seemed appropriate. Where and when two or more gathered, they had church. Church was more often dialogic rather than monologue based. People asked questions and received provocative answers from Jesus. Worship was a shared experience, not a performance by the few for the many. A core group of disciples trained to become leaders and teachers, and they gained their own followers over time. There were no restrictions on who could come and listen, so it was perfectly fine for prostitutes and thieves and soldiers and killers and even Gentiles to participate. There was a very clear understanding that the good news was a gift, and the people who needed it most were the people who needed it most. Jesus gave the mutually exclusive impression that each person was the most important person in the world and the least important. Everywhere Jesus went, some accepted him, while others rejected him. It was just the way things worked—some people were saved, some were not; some chose to follow, some went home; and some sinned no more others sinned as much as before.

There is good evidence that were Jesus to visit us today, he probably would not spend much time in any of our churches. If he entered our temples at all, he might stand before our pulpits and point out to us all the Pharisaic and scribal practices that we proudly proclaim as Christianity. It is highly likely that he might present us with a Bible and ask if we've ever read it. On his way to be with the people on the streets, he might stop in our bookstores and coffee shops to upturn the tables and drive the baristas out with a whip of cords. I'm reaching here, but I have a sneaking suspicion he might not be amused by what we've done to his church.

At the same time, I believe he would look with love and compassion at our hearts and readily forgive all our transgressions. He is very good at this—lucky for us. I doubt that he would label what we do as evil, but it is still a far cry from good. It is almost impossible to escape what we have become. It is unreasonable to expect us to abandon our buildings, discontinue our programs, fire our paid professionals, and give away our wealth to poor people. It didn't happen widely the first time Jesus was here; it isn't going to happen now.

But we need to critically examine what we are doing and why we do it. We need to ask whether there might not be a better way. We need to evaluate our priorities and clarify our purposes—and do everything in our power to align our actions with our God-given vision and values. We are doing many good and wonderful things, but we could do all of them better, and to do better, we've got to stop doing some things altogether.

The World Still Needs the Church

As much as the world has changed in the past two thousand years, so very much has stayed the same. People still suffer. They treat one another in cruel, hateful, and disrespectful ways. Many attempt to settle their differences with violence. Nations wage war against nations. Greedy people take advantage of poor and powerless people. The mighty oppress the weak. Bigotry and prejudice cause us to devalue and despise those different from us. Each one of Jesus' teachings on love, grace, forgiveness, mercy, compassion, kindness, or justice is as relevant today as it was to his original audience. Nothing significant has changed. We desperately need *good news*.

The church *exists* to share the good news.

There is nothing more important for the church to do than to share the good news. Christian people have been forgiven, blessed, and given a second chance. We should do no less for every person we meet. It is time for the church of Jesus Christ to repent—to turn away from any practice that is hurtful, hateful, divisive, or damaging, and turn again toward the redeeming love of Jesus the Christ.

The Church Still Needs the World

Without a broken world, we essentially have no reason to exist. The privilege, challenge, and call to be the body of Christ for the world mean that we exist to serve. Without someone to serve, we are irrelevant. We can't afford to despise the world and to hate anyone in it. That is why unjust war, genocide, capital punishment, and other forms of final judgment must be rethought—they permanently close the door on our reason for being. The entire global community is our mission field, including those we dislike and disagree with.

But a mission field is very different from a battlefield. We go forth in the name of Christ not to win but to serve. Our tribal, primitive past offered us the metaphor of conquering Christian soldiers, filled with militaristic and violent imagery of winning the war for salvation. By God's grace and spirit we have evolved into more enlightened times, learning that reconciliation and peace are much more powerful than destruction and slaughter. Today, we seek the kind of unity and connection glimpsed in the Pauline Letter to the Ephesians.[1] We do not fight to eliminate our enemies, but we embrace them and offer them a share of the treasure we have received. We come bearing gifts, not weaponry. We seek to love our enemy, not destroy him or her.

What a pitiful and boring place this would be if everyone agreed. It is apparent from our Scriptures that there will always be some who reject the love of God, the gospel of Jesus Christ, and the right hand of fellowship. It is also clear that there will be divisions within the body of Christ. What isn't so clear is why. One reason may simply be that we are stuck. As much as we talk about the guidance of the Holy Spirit and divine revelation, too many of us are literalistic and close-minded people of the Book. Some Christians are entrenched in the Hebrew Scriptures, which contain stories and instructions that tend to be more legalistic, punitive, tribal, and primitive. The judgment of God supersedes the mercy of God for these believers. It is incomprehensible that so many Christians prefer "an eye for an eye, a tooth for a tooth" to "love God with all your heart, mind, soul, and strength, and love your neighbor as yourself," but many obviously do, since their faith perspective is fundamentally pre-Christian and focused on the more vengeful attributes of God. Those who ground their faith in the New Testament often do so legalistically, giving preference to the instructions of Paul over those of Jesus. Even a Pauline-based Christianity would be more grace filled if we arranged his letters (and those written in his name by others) in chronological order instead of longest to shortest. Paul's thinking and theology evolved over time, and he grew from a provincial, pietistic church planter to honor the teacher Jesus into a visionary evangelist calling for a global faith in a cosmic Christ. The Gospel writers—and those today who base their Christianity in the Gospels—focused more on the message and the miracle of the resurrection than on the messenger. Jesus was a vessel through which God poured out the Holy Spirit on the world. The risen Christ confirmed that this process did not end with his passing but was a vital, vibrant, timeless flow through the ages. God did not stop speaking when the process of canonization reached its conclusion in the fourth century.

Jesus taught his followers, and so we learn today, that they were to be perfect, that they were not to judge, that they were to be as pure as children, that they were to be servants, that they were to love one another, and that they would do even greater deeds than Jesus himself.[2] These things happen not because we try really hard to be good; they happen because God makes them happen in us as we live faithfully and fully for God's glory.

Does the Church Still Need Us?

The world needs the church, and the church—by its very definition—needs the world, but the more painful and pertinent question is this: does the church need us? It depends on how we define *church*. If we mean buildings and programs and publishing houses and denominations and television ministries, then of course the church will need human drones to prop up the organization and make sure the machinery doesn't break down. But if that's how we use most of our time, we really don't have time to be the real church. The church simply isn't about us.

Trend watchers and cultural analysts have identified a fascinating shift—Christianity is moving south. For the past two thousand years, Christianity has been defined by the values, beliefs, and worldviews of the Northern (and predominantly Western) Hemisphere. In our near future, the majority Christian population will live south of the equator.

The Southern Hemisphere houses the largest portion of the world's population, contains the most developing (and underdeveloped) nations, experiences the highest birth and death rates, battles the worst poverty, disease, and domestic violence, and still operates from a primarily premodern worldview. The global Christianity to come will be radically different from the Christianity of the United States. What we have so long assumed to be the right way to do things will be rejected by millions of African, Asian, and South American followers of Jesus Christ.

Human history is a series of ups and downs. Nations and movements develop and grow, settle into a time of prosperity and comfort, ride the rising expansion of the bubble, and assume it will last forever. This sense of security is a sham—the bubble always bursts. (Think of the parable of the wealthy farmer who built up barns to store his bountiful harvest—known as the parable of the Rich Fool, Luke 12:13-21.) We, in America, have had it good for a long, long time, but there is evidence that we have taken much for granted.

Christianity grew in a time of oppression and persecution. It holds a special appeal for abused, enslaved, impoverished, and marginalized persons. Indeed, Christianity is not really designed for affluent, powerful, and complacent persons. Many people never truly value what they have until they lose it. This truth is especially sad because it doesn't need to be this way.

We have much to learn from history. We can remind ourselves that the church isn't about rules and regulations and property and prosperity. We can remember that Christianity is not intended to be one more way to divide us from them, to separate people into haves and have-nots. We can see that there is no place in authentic discipleship for huge egos, unchecked ambition, destructive competition, and accumulation of creature comforts. We can comprehend that the issues that seem so massive and important today fade into insignificance as we grow up and grow in love.

The church still needs us because God still loves us and wants us to love the world. God wants us to take up the mantle of Christ— to put away childish and hurtful things, to put on compassion, love, mercy, and kindness, to get up off our pews and get out of our buildings, not to invite people to church, but to *be* the church—and to be Christ incarnate for a broken and suffering world.

Notes

1. "He is our peace; in his flesh he has made both groups into one and has broken down the dividing wall, that is, the hostility between us. He has abolished the law with its commandments and ordinances, that he might create in himself one new humanity in place of the two, thus making peace, and might reconcile both groups to God in one body through the cross, thus putting to death that hostility through it" (Eph 2:14-16).
2. Matthew 5:48, 7:1-5; Mark 10:13-16; Luke 22:24-27; John 15:12-13, 14:12.